CATCHING LAKE TROUT

CATCHING LAKE TROUT

John Gale

THE BOYDELL PRESS

First published 1990 by The Boydell Press, Woodbridge

The Boydell Press is an imprint of Boydell & Brewer Ltd
PO Box 9, Woodbridge, Suffolk IP12 3DF

ISBN 0 85115 267 8

British Library Cataloguing in Publication Data
Gale, John
1. Trout & salmon. Fly fishing
I. Title
799.1755
ISBN 0-85115-267-8

This publication is printed on acid-free paper

Printed in Great Britain by
St Edmundsbury Press, Bury St Edmunds, Suffolk

CONTENTS

To Do'

ACKNOWLEDGEMENTS

I offer my sincere thanks to the following, without whose help and encouragement, this book would not have been written.

To Peter Thomas, international trout angler extraordinary, who first encouraged me to write about trout fishing.

To Chris Dawn and Steve Windsor, for their help and guidance, and for allowing me to use extracts from articles that first appeared in their excellent *Trout Fisherman Magazine*.

To Tom Johnson of the award winning Anglia Photoworks, Cambridge, and his son Steve for their assistance with my photography and film processing.

To my fishing pals who, by their friendship and direction, have helped me learn the angling lessons that have enabled me to write this book and get it published.

To my late father, my mother and my sister for their lifelong encouragement and inspiration.

And, finally, to my lovely, long-suffering wife, Dora, and our family, for enduring for some years my love affair with the beautiful Rutland Water and other trout lakes, and the many hours of loneliness my fishing, and writing about it, has caused.

Peter Thomas (foreground – International trout angler extraordinary

FOREWORD

I met John Gale through my honorary membership of the Cambridge based Invicta Fly Fishing Club. He had written an article in the club's newsletter, which I thought was full of original thinking.

This prompted me to suggest that he should approach one of the fishing magazines with a view to having them publish his ideas and experiences.

He has subsequently written this book. Blameworthy and flattered, as indeed I am, he has asked me to write a brief foreword.

Most fly-fishermen would admit to specialising, to some degree, in a particular style and method. John's success and reputation is built on his all-round ability and willingness to adapt to the most suitable style and method for the particular situation and prevailing conditions. His double-sided fly-box bears true witness to this fact – from double tandem monsters, to rows of orderly and comparatively small nymphs. He would admit, that given the right circumstances, the method that gives him most pleasure is fishing very small nymph patterns on a floating line, from an anchored boat. To witness that, can be a revelation!

One of John's characteristics, and one that obviously gives him considerable pleasure, is the generous sharing of his expertise, knowledge and flies.

It is the collective resources of our education and actual fishing experience that the 'thinking' angler will apply when translating or seeking an explanation for his success or failure. It is from this analysis that we hope to go forward and thus improve both our success and pleasure.

None of us, including John, would dare to be so presumptuous as to claim that we had found the real answer to explain all the various phenomena and circumstances that occur in a particular fishing situation. Individual anglers will develop their own plausible pet theories, ideas and 'prejudices', which satisfy their personal curiosity. It is upon the foundation of this knowledge that we draw and add to every time we go fishing, or read an article or book.

This book is John's unique interpretation of his experience, which I feel we can readily, and usefully, add to our own.

Peter Thomas
June 1989

INTRODUCTION

Trout fishing, over the years, has given me such affinity with nature and the countryside, that I no longer go out to the lake with just the thought of catching trout on my mind, although that, naturally, still has a high priority.

The blue haze carpeting the May woodland, the raucous call of a pair of migrating snow geese and the dangling gold brush of the afternoon fox are examples of the many and varied sights and sounds that accompany me whenever I'm fishing one of our country's big lakes. A day's trout-fishing, approached in the right manner, is a therapy that, in my view, does more good than would ten visits to a psychiatrist. It provides the cheapest 'medicine' that money can buy.

Yet, paradoxically, I still dream of catching that elusive double-figure trout, and seldom sleep well on the night before a day at the lake, my thoughts full of where and how I'll fish on the morrow. And all this, after the thrill of the capture of more than ten thousand trout over a long career, the largest an 8lb 2oz 'wild' rainbow, from Grafham in June 1980.

Writing has given me an opportunity to put something back into a sport that has provided me with so much pleasure over the years. I hope, in its reading, you will find in this book that elusive something to not only improve your own enjoyment of trouting, but to help fill your basket as often as mine, to the consummate satisfaction of my family and friends, who rate big-lake trout the culinary equal to Scottish salmon.

The anecdotes are included in an attempt to make the volume something more than just another 'how to do it' book on trout fishing. Although I have endeavoured to spell out most of the lessons I have learned over the years, I've also tried to put together some pages you will find enjoyable as light bedtime reading. The exciting, memorable or humorous moments are all true. Only the names of the people have been changed, 'In order to protect the innocent', as the saying goes.

One of the things you will notice about the book is the relative absence of flies and fly-patterns. It's not that I don't set great store by the flies I use. I do. But if the truth is to be told I probably only use ten different patterns for ninety per cent of my fishing time, albeit in various hook sizes and different dressings, to give them more, or less, buoyancy. I include photographs and tying instructions for these patterns. I also own up to having a large, four-tier fly box and several smaller fly boxes full of different offerings. This is because I spend many of my winter evenings at the fly vice and love making up new patterns. However, most of them get no, or very little, use. When the chips are down I always seem to plumb for those flies, nymphs and, occasionally, lures that have proved successful in the past. Presentation is, to me, far more important than the hook covering and my flies often look so shabby that I frequently get a refusal when offering one to a fellow angler. Not, I admit, that colour doesn't sometimes seem to be important. It does, particularly in the harder fished areas of the lake. But if I were restricted to a black or white lure, a lime green, black or pheasant tail nymph and a few different coloured sedge imitations, I'd be confident of catching trout on most occasions.

So good reading, tight lines and happy outings. What more could I wish anyone.

Chapter One

PRESENTATION: THE BASICS

Trout are voracious feeders, when provided with an ample, freely available food source. Pound for pound they put on weight faster than pigs in special rearing pens. So why, at times, are they so difficult to catch?

The answer is, usually, that we haven't employed the basics of presentation that apply to all branches of fishing:

> Get the bait, or, in our case, the fly, to the fish, at the taking depth, drifting it, with the stream, in a manner that resembles the trout's natural food form.

This is, of course, much easier to say than to accomplish. It is, however, something we must always remember when at or on the water. Indeed, if we are to continually put trout in our basket, we have only to ensure we are fishing over fish and are applying the rules of good presentation. More of that important issue, fish location, later. For the moment, let's consider the basic principles of fly presentation.

Presenting the fly at the taking depth implies that trout, like all fish, feed at different levels in the water. Those of you who started your angling in the ranks of the country's three million-odd coarse fishermen, will know that moving a float up and down a cast often results in bites that would, otherwise, not be forthcoming. Fish do seem to feed in certain strata in the water and will only consume food particles that appear in that layer of water. Maybe this has something to do with water temperature. I don't know. Frequently, however, bait placed two or three inches up or down from this feeding level results in the fishes' complete rejection of the offering. Trout undoubtedly behave in a similar fashion, for much of the time, so the matter of depth of fly presentation is of paramount importance, if we want to succeed in their deception.

In recent years, the fishing tackle manufacturers have helped make our task easier by producing a wide range of sinking lines. These enable us, with correct technique, to fish our flies not only at different depths but, just as importantly, at different trajectories in the water. Watch a water-butt full of nymphs at the bottom of your garden, if you have such

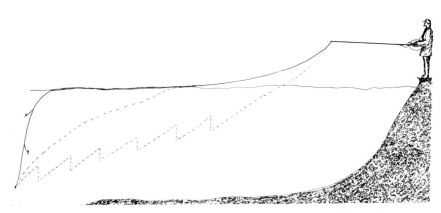

Floater and team of nymphs, the point fly leaded. The dotted lines show the difference in trajectory when the continuous figure-of-eight retrieve or the pause-and-draw type of retrieve is employed

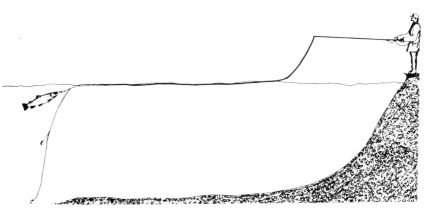

The Floater presents the 'bob' fly to trout feeding near the surface

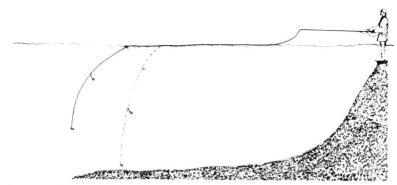

The buoyant fly on the top dropper keeps the leader higher in the water than a conventional cast (see dotted line)

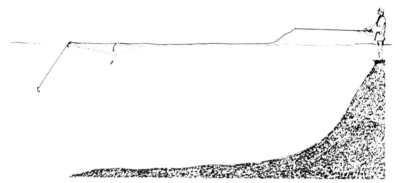

The buoyant fly on the middle dropper keeps only the top of the leader high in the water. The top dropper sinks and rises with a paused retrieve

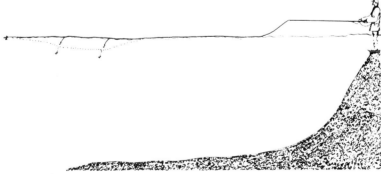

The buoyant fly on the point keeps the leader high. The dotted line shows how the middle and top droppers sink on pausing the retrieve. They rise again on the draw

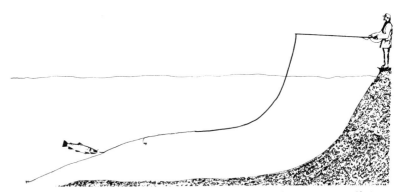

The Wetcel 1 slow-sinker presents the flies to trout feeding just off the bottom, in deep-water swims

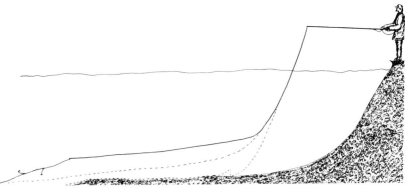

Wetcel 1 line, showing the difference in retrieval path when continuous figure-of-eight retrieves or the pause-and-draw type of retrieve is used

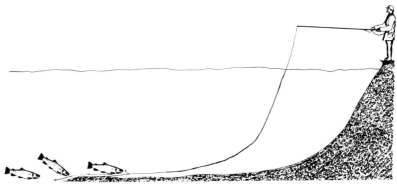

The Wetcel 2 line gets the flies to bottom-feeding trout, in deep water

The Intermediate line will 'cover' the mid-water feeders

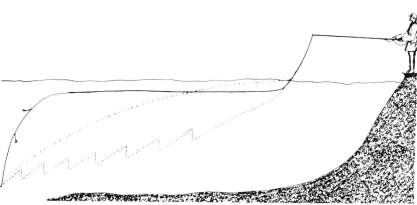

The Intermediate line. The dotted lines show the different trajectories of
the flies, using the figure-of-eight continual retrieve and the retrieve-and-
pause methods

a thing. The hectically twisting, gyrating mosquito pupae kick their way upwards for a few inches, then drop down a little before kicking on up again. Our nymphs can be presented in this manner, too, with a little thought. The diagrams clearly show what I mean.

I'll deal, in a later chapter, with fly creation and its application so far as presentation is concerned. Suffice to state, at the moment, that flies with varying buoyancy will fish in different ways, whatever fly-line is employed, and we have to consider the impact this may have on the way our artificial food-form may appear to the trout.

When using a floating fly-line, if we put a very buoyant fly on the point of our leader, with two light flies further up the cast, the point fly will keep in the surface film. The other two flies will sink, slightly, below the surface if left alone. As soon as we start to retrieve, however, the buoyant point-fly will help lift the other flies towards the surface film. When we stop retrieving again, they will fall, once more, below the surface film.

The same set-up, fished on a sinking line, would cause the flies to fish in a very similar fashion except they would be several feet sub-surface after the weight of the fly-line had dragged them down, and they would move down in the water on retrieval and rise again, slightly, at each pause: exactly the opposite movements to those made with the floating-line, yet paradoxically the same rise and fall effect the natural nymphs make on their journey to the surface.

Let's take a closer look now at that most widely used line of all, the floater. This line can be used to present flies at depths varying from nought (i.e. the surface film) to twenty feet. As the diagram shows, however, the type of retrieve used makes all the difference to the depth at which the artificials will fish, and the way they behave in the water. A continuous figure-of-eight retrieve will keep the flies moving, for instance, in a much higher plane in the water than a draw and pause type of retrieval. We can make our nymphs behave a bit like the mosquito pupae in the water-butt if we first let our artificials sink, then retrieve them with a couple of figure-of-eights, before pausing for two or three seconds, then figure-of-eighting again – and so on, keeping to the general pattern but changing the timing, to keep the retrieval irregular.

To make our flies fish on, or very near, the surface we must, in some way, carry the floating qualities of the fly-line through to the artificial. This can be achieved in several different ways. A chemical floatant called Gink can be applied to our leaders, and/or flies, to keep them up in the water. A buoyant fly suitably positioned on the leader will have a similar effect. Fishing one, two or three flies on our cast changes the way the fly or flies behave, and the speed of retrieve will dramatically change their depth of presentation.

It is very important to think out, and always be aware of, the depth our flies are fishing so that, in the event of a 'take', we can repeat the medicine to continue catching. If we are fishing deep, with any line, a 'count-down' before, and sometimes during, a retrieval is the most systematic and satisfactory method of obtaining this information. It also helps us to maintain concentration whilst fishing. I'm sure we have all, at some time or another, had our rod nearly wrenched out of our hands whilst our minds wandered, only to end up fishless and dejected. Sod's law says the minute you stop concentrating, a fish will offer itself to the slaughter. I can remember a hundred such instances in my angling career, nearly all of them ending in utter frustration and blue air!

There was one occasion, however, when lack of concentration had just the opposite effect. It was in June 1980, at Grafham Water. The previous evening I'd been fishing in a boat off the G-marker buoy. Our limits were achieved in only two hours on the lake and some of the fish were in the 2lb plus range. Over a pint in the nearby Wheatsheaf I decided to try the G-marker shore early next morning.

Leaving my tackle in the car overnight I set off for the lake just before first light. It was a cloudy morning with a very strong westerly wind blowing straight down the lake. Taking my tackle from my boot I realised, to my horror, that my waders were missing. To this day I don't know if I forgot to pack them or my twenty-two-year-old son 'borrowed' them. When I next looked for them, they were hanging up in their usual place in the garage! Anyway, without them I was certainly not going to fish the G-marker area, much of which is quite shallow. I plumbed, therefore, for the dam wall. Here the wind was so strong I could hardly walk against it and I decided that casting would be impossible as the foam-topped waves crashed noisily against the concrete.

Only one place was left to fish in shoes, the boat jetty. Walking back to the car I almost decided to call it a day and go home. 'The jetty is bound to be full of anglers', I kept telling myself. 'It's a waste of time driving round there.' 'Let's go home to bed.'

Anyway, drive round there I did, and to my relief and I think amazement, there was only one angler fishing the boat harbour when I arrived. Unpacking my gear as quickly as possible, and donning my Barbour with equal haste, I made my way down to the jetty.

The other angler, a chap I hadn't met before, was fishing right on the end of the pontoon. I set my gear down as close to him as I dared, and proceeded to make up my rod. 'Done any good?' I asked politely. 'Nothing', came the curt reply. 'Too bloody windy, I think', he added.

Paying no more attention to him, I put on a floater and a leader of eighteen feet, with a single damsel-nymph which I had tied with a latex body and coloured olive with a waterproof marker pen. I sat down on the pontoon, mainly because the gale was doing its best to blow me into the water, and cast out. Tucking my rod under my arm, I allowed

The author with his 8lb 2oz Grafham rainbow, a fish of a lifetime

the nymph to settle on the lake bed before starting to inch it back. A damsel-fly larva, which I was trying to imitate, will crawl slowly over the lake bed in its search for prey, stopping frequently to inspect any likely morsel. So every ten seconds or so, I paused to let the nymph settle again, then started the retrieve again. I had just cast out for the third time, when the angler from the end of the pontoon stepped over the gear behind me, on his way off the jetty. 'I'm away', he said. 'Bloody hopeless in this wind!'

'Cheers', I returned, aloud. 'Now I can get on the end of the jetty', I thought, inwardly.

It was at this point that I noticed my towel was three parts of the way out of my tackle bag and about to be blown into the lake by the howling wind. By now it was light enough to see the boats in the sailing club harbour being tossed up and down in the water like small corks in a jacuzzi. The fishery management's blue and white cabin boat, which was moored about sixty yards in front of me, was tugging at its anchor rope in the storm. Two mallard sat huddled under the bank to my right, their feathers ruffling every now and then as another gust of wind penetrated even their shelter.

I laid my rod down on the pontoon and turned to put the towel back in my gear. My hand had no sooner touched the leather strap of my tackle bag than my reel screamed and my rod scraped its way off the jetty towards the lake! I caught it, more by luck than judgement, as the butt was about to drop off the pontoon and, as good fortune would have it, as my hand encircled the rod handle, my finger failed to catch my nylon backing, which, at this point, was running off the reel at a rate of knots I had never experienced before. Collecting my thoughts, I tried to apply pressure to the spinning reel rim with my thumb. By now my backing was almost gone and I could see the string packing appearing on the drum. There was nothing else for it than to turn the rod sideways, clamp the reel and hope for the best. By now the fish must have been past the blue and white cabin boat, the line dangerously near the anchor chain.

After a momentary application of pressure my line went slack and my heart sank. 'Lost it', I thought, and dejectedly began to wind the backing onto my reel, rod held high against the wind. I'd got about thirty yards back on my reel when I noticed the nylon in the water in front of me suddenly tighten. The next thing I remember is my rod bending again, and then I had to release backing again as the fish, still applying incredible pressure, made off upwind and, luckily, just clear of the jetty.

I scrambled to my feet and set the rod on its side as the backing neared its end again. The fish turned and as I ripped line back with my left hand, two feet at a time, it headed back towards me and, thankfully even further out in the lake. 'Now,' I thought, 'I'll have you.'

It was some time before I could get backing back on my reel again, but the wind was doing me a favour by blowing the loose nylon out over the water, thus preventing it from tangling, which would have been a disaster. I played that fish for what seemed an eternity, but the six and a half pound Racine-Tortue leader, and the Partridge 10 long-shank held firm. Actually, only twenty minutes had elapsed when I was ready to net the trout but as I looked round for assistance I realised I was on my own. The other fellow had gone. Surely he must have heard my reel scream . . . but then, I realised, in that wind it was hard to hear your own thoughts. With the gale doing its utmost to keep the fish from me, I gradually got it over my net and safely up onto the pontoon. It was a hen rainbow, bright as a silver salver and deep as a bream. 'About six pounds', I mused, excitedly, as I applied the priest and put it into my fish bag. 'I'll weigh it as soon as the bailiff arrives', I thought. 'It might be the best fish of the month.'

Some hours later, as Grafham bailiff Mick Bass and a few onlookers

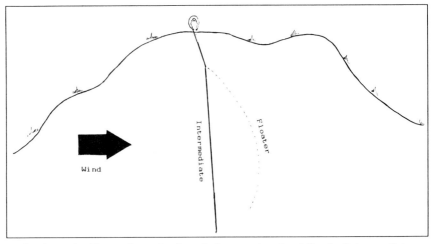

See how the Floater bows in the wind on retrieval, whilst the Intermediate stays straight, beneath the wind-drift

put the twenty-six-inch rainbow on the scales, we realised that, at 8lb 2oz, this was not only the fish of the month, it was the fish of a lifetime: the second largest ever taken from that fabulous fishery and one whose plaster cast still hangs over the bar in the fishing lodge. It had been my lucky day. If I'd had waders in the car I wouldn't have fished on the jetty. If my hand had caught my nylon backing on the fish's first run it would have undoubtedly broken me. If the fish had turned under the pontoon I'd almost certainly have lost it round the anchor chains. Several thousand fish later it's still my best 'wild' trout. Perhaps I'll never be as lucky again.

The intermediate line, a relatively recent innovation, has been a Godsend to those of us who like to fish nymphs and who find fishing a floater in a cross-wind so frustrating. At such times, prior to the introduction of the intermediate line, the resistance imparted by the wind forming a bow in the floating line caused trout to reject our flies before we could make contact with them.

I remember one such incident, soon after I bought my first intermediate. I was fishing off the Normanton shore at Rutland, over a huge shoal of stock and overwintered rainbows. The fish were mopping up buzzers in the relatively shallow water and were easily located because every now and then a splashy rise would disturb the heavy ripple that the fresh north-westerly breeze was forming on the face-wind bank. We anchored our boat about fifty yards off-shore, there being no bank anglers to contend with, and both made up floaters with a team of three nymphs on a twenty-foot leader. My partner had an offer, first cast, the bowed fly-line visibly moving a full yard as a trout struck his artificial. He struck, with rod high but made no contact. It was my turn next, but my similar 'offer' was also missed despite what I thought was a lightning response as I tried to tighten into the fish. Moments later my pal missed another and began to curse.

I immediately wound in my line until the join with the leader was inside the bottom ring of my rod, broke the join, changed reels to the one holding my new intermediate line and rejoined the cast. The change had been so quick my friend hadn't even noticed.

On the first cast with this new set-up, I tucked my rod under my arm to let the leader and nymphs settle and it was almost wrenched out of my hands as a lively rainbow of about one and a half pounds hooked itself and made a spirited bid for freedom. 'What did you get that on?' my pal enquired. 'Green and Brown nymph', I truthfully replied. 'I've got one of those on,' he returned, 'but I can't touch them. I'm getting lovely takes, but can't hook them. Can I borrow your hook-hone?' I duly obliged. It made no difference, as I suspected. At midday, when we decided to adjourn for lunch, I had boated fourteen superbly fit rainbows to my frustrated friend's blank. Only once had he succeeded in hitting one of his many 'takes' and that fish shook the hook-hold at the net.

After lunch, at my suggestion my partner bought an intermediate line from the small tackle shop at the lake – the new management have a much larger shop now, where you can purchase everything from a Barbour to a boot-liner, all at discount prices. I fitted the line to one of his spare spools that already had some backing on it and needle-knotted a tippet piece to the end of the line.

We purchased second tickets and set off to our mark in eager anticipation. Even as we anchored up we could see fish still showing occasionally and, as my mate prepared to cast with his new acquisition, I took a fish, 'on the drop', with my first cast.

We left the lake that afternoon having boated our full complement of thirty-two trout, all rainbows, at 4.30p.m. By then my pal had caught eight, honours being almost even during the afternoon session. This proved conclusively, I believe, that the intermediate line sinking below the ripple, and therefore unaffected by the wind, was helping to present our nymphs far more naturally than the floater would allow, on the day. More importantly, it had reduced to a minimum the amount of resistance being offered to the taking trout.

For bank or boat nymphing, for ninety per cent of the time, a floater or intermediate line will satisfy all your presentation requirements. Only very occasionally will you need to resort to heavier sinking lines, in order to catch. I'll deal with these instances in another chapter.

Chapter Two

THE TACKLE QUESTION

Today's all-round trout fisher needs a considerable array of tackle to cope with the many different conditions he will meet during the season, given the various methods he may wish to employ. Rods and lines must be 'matched', for optimum performance, and the tackle-bag or holder should be large enough to accommodate tackle, food and drink, and accessories like sun-glasses, drogue etc. This should not discourage the newcomer to our sport, however, as these items may be acquired over a period of several seasons. It is, though, important to have a 'tackle plan' from the start, if costs are to kept to a minimum. I know several anglers who found they had to scrap their first set of equipment in the second season because not enough thought had gone into their original choice of tackle, or they had been wrongly advised.

Even with the vast assistance available to today's trout fisher, in the form of monthly magazines, books and qualified tutors, it still takes time to get to grips with all facets of the sport. Also, it is important during the process of learning for the angler to actually catch a trout or two, as confidence is a vital ingredient for regular success. I therefore recommend that, for a few outings at least, the beginner visits one of the numerous small trout fisheries that have mushroomed in every county during the past decade. These lakes, usually just a few acres of water, are regularly stocked to give an almost permanent known head of fish and the angler can be reasonably sure that he is 'covering' fish frequently during a day's outing. His chances of catching are much higher than they would be on a big reservoir, where fish location is something of an art in itself.

Most of these small fisheries have no boat fishing available. In any event, limiting early outings to bank fishing also enables the beginner to fully exploit his every opportunity with a maximum of three different fly-lines, namely a floater, an intermediate and a Wetcel 1 slow-sinker.

Many trout fishermen find these small fisheries meet their needs totally and never venture beyond. That is their choice, of course, but I strongly recommend that the serious student of the art of fly-fishing try his hand at big-lake trouting, once a modest mastery of rod and tackle has been accomplished. The constant challenge of fishing for trout on

Shakespeare box, Sparton line-raft, Leeda Dragonfly and System 2 reels, and a box full of nymphs and lures of all kinds

a large lake is one that keeps alive one's interest in the sport, broadens one's understanding of the activity and provides access to a larder of one of nature's finest foods. Big-lake trout are widely regarded as the culinary equal to wild Scottish salmon.

Let's assume, therefore, that our plan is to start by bank-fishing on a small water, then to progress to reservoir 'banking' and, later, reservoir boat-fishing.

Since our chosen sport is very much an outdoor activity, suitable waterproof clothing is absolutely vital if we are to derive full enjoyment from our long leisure hours. A Barbour coat is worth its weight in gold during a heavy downpour, and properly treated will last for many seasons. It should have a hood. Choose a coat that offers plenty of room for several layers of pullovers underneath, to help keep out the cold on a raw day. There are some new waterproof coats on the market that claim to have benefits over the traditional waxed cottons. I cannot comment as I have never tried one. My Barbours have always given me exceptional service and I've never felt inclined to experiment further.

Waterproof over-trousers are equally important. There are many types on the market. Most of the cheaper ones cause condensation to form on the inside, if worn for long periods. Barbour over-trousers need constant re-proofing in the seat area if boat fishing is to remain a pleasurable experience in the rain. Lifeboat type oilskins are probably the best buy, but these are not cheap. As the saying goes, "You pays yer money and you takes yer chance!" I can only advise that a wet bum on a cold day is highly unsatisfactory and most uncomfortable. Piles, or 'heaps' as my friend Peter calls them, may also be the result.

Waders aren't usually important until you progress to big-lake bank-fishing. Even here there are lots of places where waders aren't necessary. Dam fishing and no-wading areas, for instance. However, not having a pair can unnecessarily restrict you on occasion. Wellington boots are essential when waders aren't worn. Buy both of these items at least one size too large to accommodate boot liners if you suffer from cold feet in winter or early spring. Some people swear by the more expensive, studded soles but, personally, I have never found the extra cost worthwhile. Ordinary cleated soles haven't, so far, let me down. Chest waders are not allowed on many waters, presumably for safety reasons. Why Water Authorities, or whoever, regard wading up to the waist in a lake as hazardous when, so far as I know, there is no restriction to fishing in chest waders on fast flowing rivers like the Spey or the Aberdeenshire Dee, I shall never understand.

Which reminds me of a true story, I must tell you.

Four of us were spending a few days at Rutland Water, in its second or third season and staying at a nearby hotel. Ian and I had decided to try boat fishing on this particular day and Pete and Graham preferred the bank. By 4p.m. Ian and I had boated our double limits in an exciting period in the North Arm, near Dickinson's Bay, on pheasant-tail Magics. As we motored home we waved to Pete and Graham as they fished the east shore of that bay. Pete held up two fingers, but I'm not sure if he was trying to tell us his score or be more explicit.

Anyway, we gutted our fish and put them in the lodge freezer, then drove back to the hotel for two hot baths.

It must have been about this time that Graham, never one to do things the ethical way in those days, decided he wanted to fish on the other side of Peter, who had just landed another two-pound rainbow. Instead of winding in, conventionally, and walking to his new station via the shore, Graham walked across in front of Pete, who was just wading out again, dragging his line behind him.

'What did you get it on, Pete?' Graham enquired.

'Pheasant-tail', came the reply.

'Were you fishing it fast, or slow?' Graham continued to question as he backed away from his pal.

'Pretty . . .' was all Pete had time to reply, as Graham stepped back into a deep channel, formerly a large ditch, and disappeared beneath the surface of the rippled water. Only his hat, a boil of bubbles and the top two sections of his rod revealed his whereabouts.

Pete burst out laughing and it was several seconds before he realised the seriousness of the situation. By this time Graham had surfaced, arms thrashing, in a frenzied attempt to get his boots onto *terra firma*.

Pete eventually got him to shore and sat him on the bank, trying to drag his mate's waders off his legs. Graham has legs with girths the size of some men's waists. Getting his waders off in normal circumstances is a job for a tug-o-war team. Wet with icy-cold water, the job proved impossible.

Graham's teeth chattered, as he shivered, like a Mexican band full of maracas, and as he squelched his way back to Pete's car the air was blue with profanities, as only Graham knows how.

Back at the hotel when we'd all, except Graham, stopped laughing we eventually got his clothes off and wrapped him in blankets from one of the beds. After a couple of brandies, which he downed despite his clicking teeth, Graham made his way to the bathroom for a shower. He'd been gone only a few minutes when a screech came from the shower-room, followed by a string of words that would have made an Admiral blush.

Next thing we saw was this huddled figure, face purple with chill, coming back into the bedroom, Mexican band playing loudly on his teeth as he stuttered, 'The . . . water's cold!'

Ian and I had used up the hotel's modest hot water supply.

Several hours and about seventeen pints later we were all laughing about the incident, Graham included, although his language hadn't improved much.

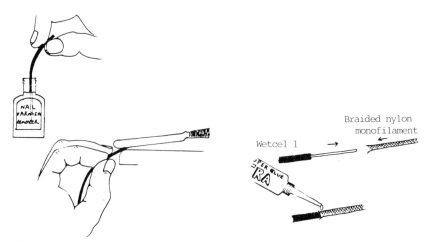

Stripping the outer skin of a shooting
head before fixing to backing line

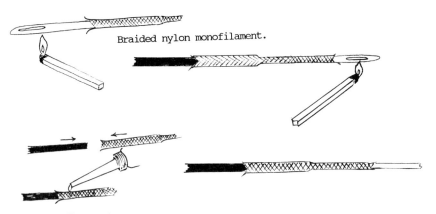

Using braided nylon to join a fly-line to
monofilament backing

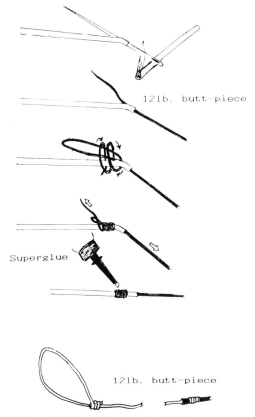

Joining the butt-piece to the fly-line

But back to the tackle question. A fishing waistcoat can hardly be termed a 'must' as far as tackle goes, but it is certainly something you should put on your birthday list. The Bob Church American-type suede finish coats are not only good-looking, they have lots of pocket space for all those fly-wallets, line-floatants and sinkers, spools of leader nylon, scissors, hook-honer, priest, sun-glasses, fishing permits and all those other items of angling clobber to which we seem to need instant access. When it's too warm to wear your Barbour, the waistcoat is the only sensible way of carrying the stuff.

On the subject of rods, I recommend you buy the best you can afford. A ten-foot carbon, with an AFTM rating of 7/8/9 will give you all the power you need to combat a face wind on a large reservoir, or punch out a long cast on opening day. Do try the rod, reel and line for comfort before you buy and make sure the reel you purchase not only holds a full line plus at least fifty yards of 30lb nylon or braided mono-filament backing, but also complements the rod for balance. For the average budget I find the Leeda Dragonfly reels an excellent purchase.

Lightweight, yet robust, it allows for speedy line-changing, using spare spools that are relatively inexpensive. For the devotee of engineering excellence the same company market the superb System Two range of reels. These are top quality, by any standards, and have such fine clutch control that playing a large fish 'on the reel' need never again be a nerve-racking experience.

Having started fly-fishing with a so-called 'mill-end' line that failed to match the rod's rating, I strongly recommend newcomers to the sport to buy the best line they can afford. I use the Aircel Ultra double taper floating line. It rides higher in the water than most, and is easier to lift-off for a switch of casting direction. When boat fishing it is superb. Avoid weight-forward floaters like the plague. They may give you added distance, but they are awkward to lift-off and seldom turn over lightly on the water. A shooting head, made with thirty-three feet of one end of a double taper, will give you extra casting distance, if required. Make up your shooting head with a braided monofilament backing. This produces a much neater join with the fly-line than can be achieved with ordinary nylon monofilament. The line drawings demonstrate how the join can best be achieved. First, take the reel end of the shooting head and dip the last two inches in a bottle of nail-varnish remover. Leave for a minute or two. Taking it out, now scrape off the outer casing of the fly-line that has been immersed, using a knife or your finger nails. Open up the braided monofilament with a needle and seal it open by heating the needle with a lighted match. Now, simply insert the flyline-butt into the braided backing and fix permanently together with super-glue.

Whether full line, or shooting head, always match the line to the AFTM rating for your rod.

There are a number of intermediate lines on the market. I use two: Masterline and Wetcel. The former is a very slow sinker indeed and fishes only just below the surface. The latter sinks about two feet. The Wetcel 1 sinking line is the only other line I use when fishing from the shore. To avoid disturbance over shallow water, restrict yourself to a double taper, or d/t, shooting head. Braided monofilament is fine for shooting heads on floaters, intermediates and Wetcel 1 lines. Don't use it for faster sinkers, because it tends not to sink too well and may affect presentation. I always use 30lb Stren nylon monofilament backing for all my fast sinking-shooting heads. The full complement of fast-sinkers needed to exploit most situations, when boat fishing comprises;

Wetcel 2 (full weight-forward, w/f, and shooting-head)
Wetcel High Speed Hi-D (full w/f and shooting-head)
Canadian lead-impregnated shooting-head
Aquasink (full w/f and shooting-head)
Five-yard Lead-core shooting-head . . .
Ten-yard Lead-core shooting head . . .

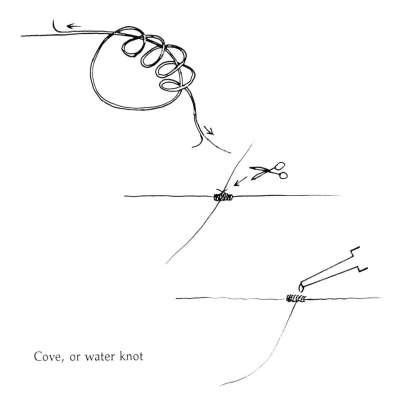

Cove, or water knot

Twenty-yard Lead-core to Stren backing
Thirty-yard Lead-core to Stren backing

All fly-lines are given a loop at the leader end, onto which the leader
is attached. I use the following methods for this exercise, which the line
drawings illustrate.

The first method I use for all lines except the lead-cores. This entails
inserting a twelve-pound nylon butt-piece into the end of the fly-line
and out again after about a quarter of an inch. This is then secured with
a needle-knot on the fly-line. A loop is tied at the leader end. The use
of the twelve-pound nylon for the butt piece ensures a nice neat knot,
which will pass easily through the smallest top eye without snagging.
The method is made much easier if the needle used to make the initial
hole in the fly-line is heated with a lighted match after insertion. This
has the effect of keeping a nice free passage for the nylon to pass up
the fly-line, before needle-knotting.

The second method I use for all lead-core leader loops, and for
lead-core to Stren-backing joins. A four-inch length of monofilament

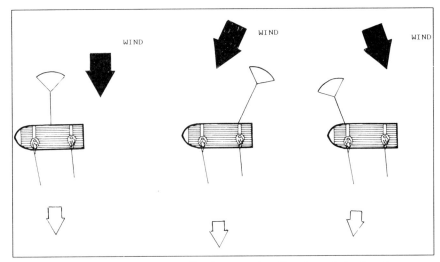

Moving the drogue dramatically changes the direction of the boat's drift

The spoon, an essential part of the trout fisherman's equipment.
Photo by kind courtesy of *Trout Fisherman Magazine* and Peter Gathercole

braid is opened and sealed using a heated needle for about two inches and the lead-core line inserted, held with a dab of super-glue and whipped with fine thread. The other end of the braid is then opened and sealed, as before, and the Stren, or twelve-pound nylon loop material, inserted. This is also held with a dab of super-glue and whipped with the same thread. I give the whipping a coat of vinyl varnish to complete the job.

Having tried many different leader materials over the years, I now use Drennan Double Strength nylon exclusively. I use it in strengths from five- to ten-pounds breaking strain. Provided you are prepared to super-glue the dropper-knots, you should have no fear that its exceptional fineness will let you down. Droppers are tied using the cove, or water-knot (see diagram) and a small dab of super-glue is applied to each knot. My usual set-up is six feet between fly-line and top dropper, four feet between top and middle dropper, and eight feet from the middle dropper to the point fly. Extra depth is achieved by lengthening the distance between the top dropper and the fly-line. super-glue has cured an earlier problem presented by this particular nylon, when fish frequently escaped, by breaking free, if hooked on a dropper.

To de-grease my leaders I use the time-honoured recipe of Fullers Earth mixed with washing-up liquid, or glycerine, if you prefer. Gink is, I find, the perfect floatant for leaders or flies.

My tackle-bag is, in fact, a box. The Shakespeare fishing-box keeps my tackle dry and is large enough to hold my reels, fly-boxes, drogue, priest, G-clamp, leader spools, sun-glasses, towel, food and drink and my waterproofs. It makes a perfect seat for boat or bank-fishing and, even when full, is easy enough to carry with its strong shoulder strap. If I plan a long walk, when bank-fishing, I usually take out the tackle I won't need, to lighten the load.

There are many different types of landing nets available on the market today. Choose one that has a large net – you never know when you're going to hook a ten-pounder – and a handle that is at least five feet long when extended. Sparton, of Nottingham, sells nets with the old-fashioned-style twisted mesh that, they claim, hooks tend not to catch up in.

The same firm markets quite the best line-tray I've come across. Made well from a cycle inner-tube, it can be attached, with the cords supplied, to the waist or leg. This will greatly assist casting, when wading, especially with sunk lines and shooting heads.

With regard to fly-boxes, I've been through a number of phases in my fishing career. I started with a couple of small boxes that were just too large to fit into a pocket. After starting to tie my own flies I found these small boxes were inadequate and bought a large, three-tier effort. This proved too cumbersome to carry and I ditched it in favour of a collection of small, pocket-size fly-boxes. These had the advantage of

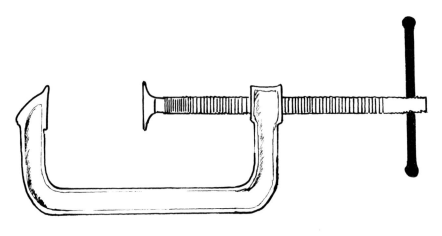

The G-clamp

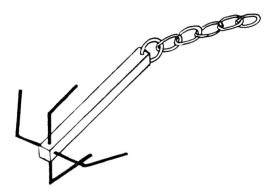

An anchor made with welded angle-iron, like the one illustrated, will
hold bottom in any wind. The 'legs' are made of softish metal bar, to
allow extrication from snags

being easily carried but were so small, I needed two boxes for nymphs, two for sedge-patterns, another for pheasant-tails, and so on. Whenever I made an evening bank-trip and just took one or two boxes with me, I found the taking pattern was in one of the boxes I'd left in the car!

Now, I've compromised. I keep all my patterns in a large, three-tiered box again. This, incidentally, fits easily into my Shakespeare box, and I have one small pocket-size box in which I keep a selection of nymphs, sedge-pupae, pheasant-tails, magics and other oddments, so that on an evening's bank-fishing trip I need only take the small box.

Drogues aren't always available on boats and those that have them usually have them bolted to the side of the gunwales, making it impossible to adjust the drift, if it becomes necessary. Better by far to have your own. This can then be fixed to any part of the boat, enabling you to alter the direction of drift at will. Mine is five feet square, with a six-inch square cut from its centre. It's made of reinforced nylon, is light, compact and dries easily. The diagrams show how differently a boat drifts when the drogue is fixed at various points around the boat.

Buy a marrow-spoon priest when you can afford it; until then a policeman's truncheon, old chair-leg or garden-dibber will do. I fished with an international angler one day in a Benson and Hedges competition and his priest was an indescribable object from a private shop. He claimed he'd found it in his wife's bedside cabinet but I never believed a word of it!

The spooning of fish should become a habit. Not only does it give you an insight into the trout's recent and past diet, it teaches you much about entomology, fish feeding habits and the ecology of the lake you're fishing. On many an occasion the spooning of a fish has caused me to change the fly I caught on for another artificial, matching the findings in the stomach contents of the captured trout. This has, several times, enabled me to bag-up much more quickly than I would have done without the spooning information.

When you start boat fishing a G-clamp is an essential part of your angling equipment. Use it to attach in position your drogue or anchor-ropes. They are then easily adjusted, if necessary, to better stabilise the drift or hang off the boat at anchor. Get one about eight inches across. It will take considerable pressure at times.

Sun-glasses are, perhaps, the most essential piece of equipment you will need, after the rod, reel, line and flies. They will protect your eyes from a mis-cast lure and from the glare of the sun. Buy the best you can afford, with polarised lenses to help you see through water. If your eyes are failing, as mine are, Bob Church markets a combined pair of Polaroid sun-glasses and magnifying insets. They are excellent.

Chapter Three

BANK FISHING: THE SMALL LAKE

The average commercial small trout fishery consists of a lake, or lakes, of less than five acres. These, because of their size and the pressure of angling, have to be managed on a 'put and take' basis. Usually, the management decide an overall stock requirement for the water, and top this up on a daily basis, according to the number of fish caught by anglers. These lakes are springing up all over the country and the competition can only be good, in the long run, for trout fishermen.

However, as with all business, profit is the motive and some fishery owners/managers are greedier than others. One famous small lake in the south of England, where charges were at the highest level, had hardly any resident stock and the management only put in as many fish as they had bookings on any particular day. The fish were of high average weight, usually with a couple of six- to eight-pound fish thrown in. Being newly stocked, and hungry, most of the daily stocking had been landed within an hour of the fishery being opened. The eight-pounder was, naturally, the envy of all but the captor, and the punters kept returning. If bookings dropped off, a well-known angler or two were invited to fish, along with a photographer, of course, and the lake was stocked to ensure not only that plenty of fish were caught, but that at least one near record breaker was in the basket! The resultant publicity ensured business for another lengthy period.

Luckily, not all fisheries are like that one, and I would say that most will give you reasonable value for money. The good, thoughtful angler will do better than the novice and the average catch will represent, in financial terms, about half the cost of the day permit. So, if a day's fishing costs £10.00 an average trouter will expect to catch about £5.00 worth of fish at stocking prices, over a period of time. As with all fishing, there will be good days and bad days, the weather playing its usual role in all this.

Some fisheries now offer trouting of a different nature. They seem to fall into two categories, both of which should serve the newcomer to our sport well, as the stocking levels are much higher than you'd find in a conventional trout lake.

The first type charge a modest fee to participate, then insist you keep

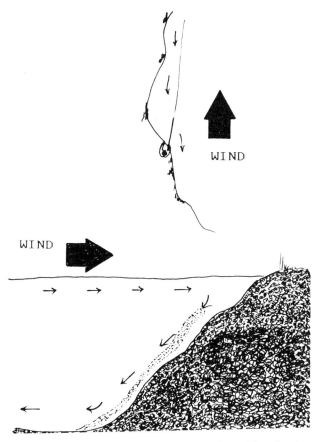

The small arrows show underwater currents depositing food on the shelf. Fish *along* the shoreline on small lakes

every fish you catch and pay for it at a retail price per pound when you leave the fishery. These fisheries are usually stuffed with fish, so take along your cheque-book. Frequently small areas are roped off so that bait-fishing on rented rod and line can be practised, usually by small boys and other members of the general public, out to catch their supper. That they serve a purpose can be judged by their popularity, but apart from being a practice-ground for the beginner, they should not attract the serious fly-fisherman. Although the fish caught obviously match the supermarket trout for taste, they bear no comparison with the big-lake fish in taste and for fighting qualities, to which you should aspire.

The other type of fishery that's likely to have an excessive head of fish in it is the 'catch and release' fishery. Here you usually pay a higher fee to participate than at the former type, and you are allowed to keep trout, if you want them, at a retail price per pound. Otherwise you may continue to catch and release at your discretion. In such a fishery it obviously pays to have high stock levels, to keep the punters coming. The only re-stocking that is needed is to replace those fish the customers purchase and a few for the herons.

If you've one of these well-stocked lakes nearby, try it for a few visits to get the feel of things. Practise the basic rules of presentation and remember the way you were retrieving when you catch. When you've got confidence in your ability to catch, and cast, try your newly acquired skills at a conventional small fishery. Here you will, undoubtedly, find the going harder, but it is a hurdle you will have to cross if you're to become a better angler.

So how do you become the average trouter, or even the good, thoughtful one?

Small fisheries, are frequently formed as a result of gravel workings or other man-made excavation. The banks, therefore, are often perched above a swiftly shelving margin where it is impossible, or unwise, to wade. These shelves are natural feeding larders for resident trout as the underwater currents carry their food and deposit it on the shelf along the lake margins. The diagrams show how this occurs and illustrate how the currents are formed, by wind action. Study these diagrams carefully and get the messages firmly implanted in your memory, for these spell out the secrets of fish location. Once you have mastered this you're more than half-way to becoming a very successful trouter, because you now know the best places to fish, even on a water with which you are unfamiliar.

Having decided that the margins are the places to concentrate on, it's a bit of a waste of time casting straight out from the shore, as most of the anglers you see will be doing. They will only be fishing the margin straight in front of them, and only then if they fish the cast right out to their feet. As the bank disturbance they have made whilst casting has probably frightened any trout from under their boots, their chances of catching will be slim indeed. Choose, rather, a shoreline where you can cast along the bank, so that you retrieve your imitations along the margins where you know the trout will be grazing. On a hard-fished water this may be difficult, but my experience has been that the face-wind shoreline usually offers an opportunity, although this may give the novice caster some problems.

Long distance casting is unnecessary on these waters but accuracy is important. Learn to cast an accurate short-line and it will be time well-spent. Set out a small car rug on your lawn, or nearby playing-field, and walk back twenty yards or so. Tie a single fly at the end of a ten-foot leader on a double-tapered floater and try to hit the rug, every time, with the fly as you practise this casting technique. When you have mastered hitting the rug relentlessly, try a plastic bucket instead. If you learn to hit that with more than half your casts, you'll be expert enough for any fishery.

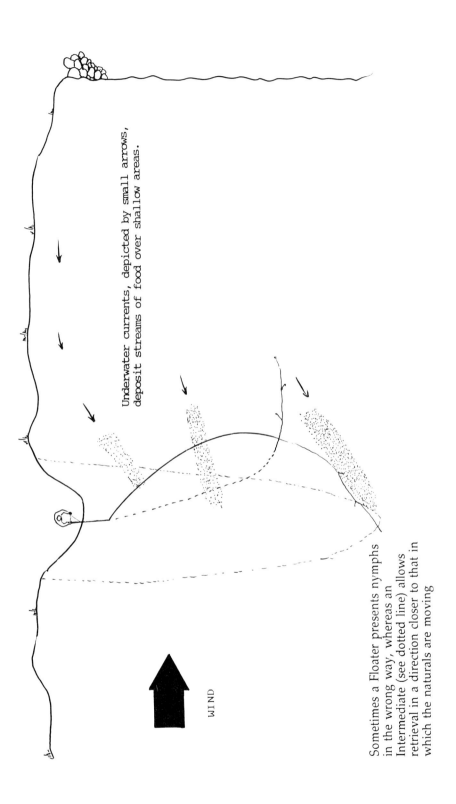

Underwater currents, depicted by small arrows, deposit streams of food over shallow areas.

WIND

Sometimes a Floater presents nymphs in the wrong way, whereas an Intermediate (see dotted line) allows retrieval in a direction closer to that in which the naturals are moving

If you're fishing the face-wind shore, as I recommend, a single fly on a ten to twelve foot leader should be about right. Fishing with more than one fly in face-wind conditions is tangle prone, even for the most experienced angler. Cast out along the shoreline so that your fly, on retrieval, is worked along the slope of the margin. If the wind is so strong that it bows your floating fly-line too much to allow you to work the margin properly, change to an intermediate line. This very slow sinker should prevent wind-action interfering with your presentation and allow you to fish your fly in the desired direction.

'But what sort of fly should I fish?' may be your next thought. This, of course, is the thousand-dollar question, which twenty years' experience would enable you to answer reasonably.

Basically, however, you should tackle these 'easy' fisheries in the way you will need to fish on the big lakes to which you should aspire. In reservoirs and the like the fish will mostly have been in the lake for quite some time, years in many instances, and they have become truly wild, feeding solely on natural sources. You must aim, therefore, to imitate that natural food form if you're to be regularly successful. Okay! I know there are anglers who catch large numbers of trout by what I call attractor methods, continually casting and stripping-in gaudy offerings that look like nothing on earth. I once spent a day in a boat on Rutland Water, fishing a competition with an international angler who spent all of the six hours allocated to us, casting out and stripping-back small 'flashers' as fast as he could go. The effort he had to put into his fishing was incredible; even I felt exhausted watching him perform in this way. Not many years ago international rules forbade fishing in this way, but these days it seems that almost anything goes as long as the flies are small and the angler refrains from standing or fishing behind the boat! Anyway, that kind of fishing is not for me. I want my days at the lake-side to be relaxed and relatively effortless. Give yourself time to enjoy the wonder of nature surrounding you, the dance of the mating great crested grebe, the dapping of the pied wagtail, and the buzz of the breeze-ruffled bullrush. Fish the imitative way, for ultimate pleasure and success.

This doesn't mean that lures are out. On the contrary. Some newly formed fisheries have an abundance of small fish, sticklebacks and the like, where a suitable imitation might well do better than a nymph. Most waters, from July onwards, have a population of small fish-fry, which increasingly begin to form a major part of the trout's diet. At these times the lure fisher can often do well. However, if you watch a shoal of small fish in the water, closely, you will realise how difficult is the perfect imitation of a darting fry. They certainly seldom swim for two feet then stop and fall tail down for a few inches before swimming another two feet, and repeating the tail-dipping descent, and so on, and so on. Yet this is how you will see many of the lure fishers retrieving their lines,

Fishing the shelf, where underwater currents deposit food. The
dotted line shows how the draw-and-pause retrieve fishes the
nymphs very slowly over the feeding area, before continuous
figure-of-eights complete retrieval

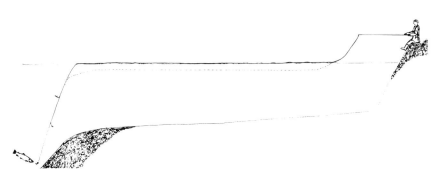

Fishing the shelf. The dotted line shows the way an Intermediate line
would beat any surface drift

relentlessly, all day. The natural fry makes much shorter trips, usually, darting up and down in the water, nose first, and from side to side. I always tie a little lead near the eye on my lures, just enough to ensure that when I stop retrieving the fry-imitation will drop in the water nose first. The dog-knobbler gives the same effect but is much heavier and therefore requires a quicker retrieve to prevent snagging. I fish my lures with short pulls of six to twelve inches, stopping, momentarily, after every fourth or fifth pull to allow the fly to sink a few inches before retrieving again. Occasionally I will try a continuous retrieve, by pulling in line slowly but continuously, with a hand-over-hand movement. This method sometimes works miraculously, as I found out one evening on the north shore of a small Cambridgeshire fishery.

Wading was allowed at this shallow end of the lake, to enable the angler to cast beyond the substantial weed-beds that lined that shore. There had been shoals of small needle-fry swimming around my feet all evening, darting here and there like a shimmering grey cloud that sparkled as the tiny fish showed their silver sides every now and then. A relatively inexperienced trouter, in those days, I had tried all kinds of lures and silvery flies, all to no avail. As dusk fell I decided to put on a small polystickle. This lure was extremely popular in those days, when the lake was full of sticklebacks and small minnows. I had tied some on to long-shank, number twelve, hooks to supplement the long-shank eights and tens which were available from local tackle dealers. As a last desperate attempt to put a rainbow in my bass, I attached one of those smaller polystickles to my twelve-foot leader. Three casts later, after deciding it was then too dark to see properly, I retreated to the bank and began reeling in, dejectedly. You've guessed the rest. Yes, the rod was nearly pulled out of my hand as a two-pound 'spotty-tail' abruptly stopped my reel in its tracks, then took off line again as it danced somewhere in the gloom.

I landed the fish, netting it with some difficulty in the twilight, and recast as quickly as I could. Tucking my rod under my arm, I began a steady hand-over-hand retrieve that kept the lure slowly but continually moving towards the shore. Half-way in and bang, another rainbow succumbed to the polystickle. I bagged up next cast to make it three in a row, and just in time to prevent a wigging from the fishery manager as he came round the lake to see why I hadn't packed up at such a late hour!

Study, if you get a chance, the underwater activity that abounds on the shelves of these small-lake margins. Grubs, caddis larvae, snails and nymphs swarm everywhere. Notice how slowly, in general, they move, often remaining stationary for periods. This is how you should fish the flies you hope will deceive the trout into thinking are natural. If you decide on a pheasant-tail nymph, for instance, let the fly settle to the lake bed after casting and then move it very slowly along the ledge,

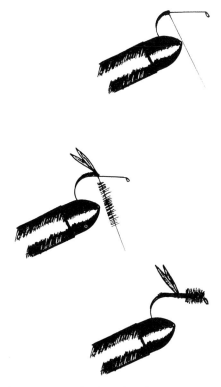

The three stages of tying the Green Magic

stopping every now and then for a few seconds before retrieving again. If you have cast out twenty yards and you are having to cast more than once every three minutes, you're probably fishing too fast. Time yourself to get a feel for what a slow retrieval really means. Ninety per cent of the anglers I watch fish their flies far too quickly, especially when nymphing.

At certain times of the day, often during late evening, fish will be seen rising all over these small fisheries. This phenomenon occurs frequently during periods of calm. It is at this time that nymphs, rising to the surface of the lake to emerge as flies, get caught in the 'bubble' of the surface film of water, just long enough for the trout to respond with avid feeding among the trapped larvae. On these occasions it may pay to fish an emergent buzzer pattern, like my 'Green Magic', keeping the nymph high up in the water by greasing your leader to within a few inches of the fly. Gink is a chemical floatant that works well for me on these occasions and I apply it in dabs every foot or so along the cast.

Learn to tie this Magic nymph. It has caught me hundreds of trout over the years and I tie it in black, green, olive, and pheasant-tail. Use fine-wire hooks to No. 12 maximum and dress them very sparsely for best presentation. The dressing is as follows.

Hook: Fine-wire, down-eyed, No. 12, 14 and 16.
Body: Slim tying-silk in black, or bright-green, or olive or cock-pheasant-tail fibres, tied round the bend and half-way along the hook-shank.
Rib: Fine gold or silver thread.
Wing: Hen blackbird fibres tied behind the large thorax, about half-way along the hook-shank.
Thorax: Matching seals'-fur or substitute.
Head: Matching tying-silk.

To demonstrate how good these flies are, let me tell you about an evening boat-session at Grafham, during the last week of June. The wind had dropped to a light southerly, and trout had started to rise everywhere. It was in the days, now sadly gone, when seemingly every yard of water on those 1,200 acres held a fish. We had tried these rising fish with all manner of patterns. As I took off my hat to select yet another offering, I noticed it was covered with small black buzzers and above my now uncovered head there were thousands. The hum of their beating wings sounded like high-powered electricity lines overhead.

I quickly changed my point fly for a No. 12 black Magic and started to cast to a fish that had risen a little way to my left. Suddenly, in the fast fading light, I thought I had become snagged on my back-cast. Without looking behind me I tried, a couple of times, to cast my line clear to cover the fish that was still moving in front of the boat. It was when my rod was almost dragged from my grasp, from behind, that I realised I had hooked a fish on my back-cast. Clearly, the Magic on the point had at some time got on, or very near to, the surface during the back-cast and a rising fish had obligingly taken it for an emergent buzzer.

I won't promise these Magics will always work such wonders, but we've so many times bagged up on them, during calm evening hatches of buzzers, that I strongly recommend you tie a few of each size and colour. I have never seen one in a shop and I have no idea of the origin of the pattern. I probably got it from some book or other. All I can tell you is, the more bedraggled you tie them, the better they seem to work.

Many of these small lakes have crystal clear water conditions for much of the year. This enables the watchful angler, wearing a good pair of Polaroids, to spot a trout swimming within casting range. With care and accuracy a fly may be presented to such a fish before it moves away, in the hope of inducing a 'take'. A leaded nymph is the fly for this job, its extra weight getting it to the area of the trout's vision much quicker than would a conventional nymph. Casting so that the fly drops through the water in the right place will take some practice, because the refraction of light through water makes the fish appear in a different place to where it actually is. A few casts, therefore, may be necessary before you get it right. Hopefully you will not have disturbed your quarry by then. Watch the fly sink towards its target and, just as it gets down to the fish's eye level, give a short sharp pull of the line. This should be just enough to move the nymph and inch or so, away from the trout. This sudden movement often induces an 'offer'. All that is now required is a gentle tightening of the line by raising the rod, to secure a firm hook-hold. This can be exciting fishing indeed.

I was once stalking a fish, which I estimated to be about four pounds, in a small lake, not far from my home, which a wealthy farmer keeps for his son and his friends. Double-figure browns and rainbows mingle here, with trout of lesser proportions.

The lake is about ten feet deep, the crystal clear water being fed from a chalk spring, further up his land. I can easily cast across it and along it, which gives you an idea of its small size. I'd spotted this brownie, nose down, grubbing along the bottom debris, on the upwind margin. Kneeling down, I watched carefully, trying to judge where to cast my leaded Green and Brown nymph, so that it would drop on his nose. Finally I made the cast and waited, with mounting excitement, as the nymph dropped perfectly towards its target. A foot to go, six inches . . .

Suddenly, from nowhere, this huge, grey shadow swept on the scene, the water whorling as the trout's swishing tail propelled it out into the lake, my nymph firmly embedded in its scissors, without me having to even raise my rod. This fish had beaten the brownie to it and it took me round and round that lake about ten times before I managed to subdue it enough to net. A full-tailed, pink-lined beauty of a rainbow that weighed nine and a half pounds, after gutting. My farmer friend told me it ate like a salmon, despite its being hand-reared from a fingerling in this small water.

I hope you enjoy similar good fortune on your small-lake venture.
Good hunting.

Chapter Four

BANK FISHING: THE BIG LAKES

Ninety per cent of the time, trout in the big lakes are conspicuous by their absence, as the saying goes. Acre upon acre of water and not a fish in sight. So how does the novice, or newcomer to the fishery, set about locating his quarry?

If you're visiting a lake for the first time and are bank fishing, the first thing you should do is speak to one of the bailiffs or other fishery staff. They are frequently trout anglers themselves, and usually have all the latest information about fish catches and the killing locations. Another fairly sure way of finding trout is to drive round the lake and look for groups of fishermen together. Check to find out if they're locals. If so, get alongside. The regulars on the lake follow the shoals relentlessly. If you're really out on your own, however, fish holding areas can be found by studying the shore and considering the wind and currents so formed.

By and large, underwater currents in a lake move in the opposite direction to the wind. However, as the line drawings show, irregularities in the shoreline, like points and bays, alter this situation. Wherever the underwater currents meet 'rising ground', that is, more shallow areas, a natural feeding area is created. The same is true where these subaqua streams come into contact with some submerged object or objects. Dead trees and hedge-bottoms come into this category. If the old hedgerow also had a ditch alongside it, this increases the 'larder' of natural food that will be deposited. Look out for areas along a bank where an undulation in the land occurs. This may be the remains of an old drainage channel or the like. Two such places come to mind, one at Grafham, on the north shore, midway between Hill Farm and Savage's Creek, the other on the Hambleton Peninsula at Rutland, looking out towards the tower in the trolling area. Both spots have produced several limit bags for me over the years, when rods on either side of me have had a leaner time. I believe that trout swim up these channels, which may only be a few inches deeper that the surrounding shore, scooping up food as they go. Inch accurate casting is sometimes necessary to put your flies where the food resides.

The author concentrates on the final lift-off

Where a point or promontory juts out into a lake, the water usually shallows up. Therefore, the area on either side and out from the point will provide a natural feeding ground for the trout patrolling the shoreline, depending on the way the underwater currents are carrying the food. If the wind is blowing right to left, fish the left-hand side of the point. If it's left to right, fish the right-hand side. If it's off your back, fish straight out from the promontory. If it's blowing straight in, both sides of the point may produce. It's important to think out where the streams will deposit the most food, and fish at those spots.

If you want to fish lures, and why not, try to select areas where small fish-fry might reside. In summer weed-beds may well provide a visual indication of where to fish. At other times of year, stick to hedge-bottoms, boat jetties, areas around dead trees and the like, for the best sport.

Of course, areas other than those mentioned will also hold fish in numbers. Flies frequently lay their eggs over deep water, where no obvious feeding ground exists. Such areas can be anywhere on the lake and may best be disregarded unless you see fish 'showing' in quantity, or you have been advised of the location by a bailiff or other benefactor. In the summer large numbers of low-flying swallows could lead you to a likely spot but, in my experience, it is not something you can be sure about.

Having decided that you are fishing in the right area, locating the depth at which the fish are feeding is the next task. This should be tackled systematically. If you have neighbours who have been successful, ask them what line and fly they're fishing. This could save you much valuable time if you have an honest, helpful angler next door. Unfortunately there are a number of trout fishermen who think it's clever to lie about their methods. I even know some who buy green floating lines in order to confuse other anglers into thinking they're using a sinker. Such conduct is to be deplored. Nothing gives me greater enjoyment than to be able to advise a nearby fisherman on a successful method or fly; even better to offer him a sample of the 'taking' pattern, and then see him also catch. This is the essence of good trouting, ensuring the prosperity of our fisheries and giving satisfaction all round.

If you're on your own, there's nothing for it but to find the taking depth yourself. First, you must decide what line you'll use. Will a floater work satisfactorily in the wind conditions that prevail? Side wind causes a floater to drift round in an arc. This is, sometimes, just what is required. However, too much drift when fishing nymphs, for instance, can cause them to fish most unnaturally and an intermediate line would be better employed in these circumstances.

Let's consider the problem if you're using a floater and fishing a lure. The length of leader and rate of retrieve will clearly allow the fry pattern to fish at a different depth. The weight or size of the offering will also affect the sub-surface path of retrieval. Cast out and begin retrieving straightaway. Next cast, count to five before retrieval, then seven, then ten and so on until you snag bottom, or catch. If you snag bottom, start over again. If you catch, remember the count and the retrieve pattern and repeat the recipe. If no 'takes' occur after twenty minutes with the floater change to an intermediate and go over the systematic 'depth sounding' retrievals again. If this brings you no luck, try the same thing with a slow-sinker. With one of these lines you should always be able to find the taking depth from the bank. Only on a dam wall are you ever likely to need a heavier sinking line; there, you might need to employ a Wetcel 2 to catch.

Occasionally, of course, trout show us their presence with some form of 'rise', splash, swirl or 'flattening' of the water. The correct interpretation of these signs is essential if we are to fully exploit the opportunities they so readily but so seldom offer us.

In calm conditions, particularly during a flat calm, trout will be seen cruising around the surface performing 'head and tail' rises among emerging nymphs that have become trapped in the surface film of water. Sometimes trout causing this particular rise form are accompanied by others with the tips of their heads pushing around the surface, in leisurely fashion, sipping up nymphs by the mouthful. The two signs can need different treatments although they often appear together in the same circumstances.

In general terms trout, like all fish, only expend as much energy as necessary when selecting a food item. If the food form they are feeding on is moving slowly the trout will, usually, move slowly to intercept it. If, however, the food-form is moving, or has the capability of moving, at speed, then the fish will often chase it vigorously, lest it should escape. Sometimes trout, 'heading and tailing', move quickly between rise patterns. At other times they have a much more casual and leisurely approach to feeding. This speed of movement gives us a good indication of the food-form being taken.

If you see fish moving fast between rises, it's a fair bet that they are feeding on hatching sedge pupae, or other large species of emergent pupae. If the trout are moving slowly between rises, they are probably taking buzzer nymphs. If you spot one of the fast-moving fish early enough on its journey towards the water covered by your cast, it may be possible to judge the speed at which it is travelling. This is important. You need to cast sufficiently in front of a rise for your fly to appear in the trout's area of vision, just before it arrives on the scene. If you get it right, you'll succeed in tempting your quarry nine times out of ten. Sedge pupae patterns seem to work best for me with these rise forms. Spooning will often disclose why. When there is a massive buzzer hatch on the water some trout, having gorged themselves on buzzers, seem to like to search out the larger sedge pupae among them, travelling at speed to do it.

The trout which spend their time 'sipping' up the buzzers, as they slowly nose or 'head and tail' their way around, need a different approach, and are generally, I have to say, quite difficult to catch. This is because they only seem to appear in this rise form when the buzzer hatch is well under way. Little surprise, therefore, that amongst the millions of natural nymphs, our artificials are ignored. Fish feeding in this particular way seldom move in a discernible direction, turning here and there as they scoop up their prey. Interception is, therefore, extremely difficult. Since we also have to fish our nymphs right in the surface film, when the tendency is for them to either float on it or sink beneath it, it is little wonder that success is a rarity on these occasions. I have had the pleasure of deceiving a trout a few times during these rises by fishing a 'suspender' buzzer. These flies are tied with a small ball of Etherfoam at the eye. The Etherfoam keeps the nymph buoyant and it can be given movement by lightly tapping the rod with your free hand after casting. Do not retrieve unless it is to recast to a new area of water.

Another pattern worth trying at these times is the Magic nymph, fished on a greased-up leader.

There is often a period, just as the main buzzer hatch dies down, when a team of suspender buzzers, Magics or Sedge Pupae will deceive a fish or two as they look to mop up the last of the hatch. This period is, unfortunately, usually short-lived.

In July the 'sipping' and 'head and tailing' rise forms can sometimes be caused by trout feeding on small, migrating snails, and I have known swans to bring about this phenomenon when feeding in weed-beds at this time of year.

I was fishing the Church Cove area at Grafham one midsummer afternoon. There was hardly a ripple on that warm, overcast day. Quite suddenly, a massive rise began, well within casting distance. The fish were either 'nosing and tailing' or 'sipping', and moving very slowly. I decided they were after buzzers and fished a team of three suspender buzzers for half an hour, without result. About fifty yards to my left and upwind, a group of about six swans were feeding avidly in the weed-beds. I watched them for some time before the thought occurred to me that they might be moving small snails that were then floating downwind on the surface and offering the trout a leisurely opportunity to gorge themselves. I quickly tied on a team of three Floating Snail patterns and cast these among the rising fish. Although I could clearly see my imitations on the surface and occasionally saw a trout inspect the offerings, I had not a single 'offer'.

'Too many naturals', I thought and, walking up the bank towards the

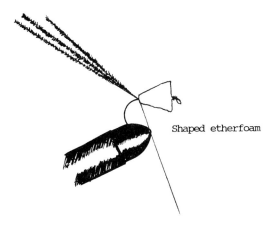

Shaped etherfoam

Tying the floating snail imitation

swans, I began throwing stones at them, moving them out into the lake and away from the weed-bed.

'You should be ashamed of yourself', a passing lady chastised. 'Those poor swans have more right to the water than you have.'

She was, of course, right, but I didn't bother trying to explain my motive; I wanted to get back to the fishing.

It was a full five minutes later that I had my first take, a confident pull following a sipping rise to the middle of my three snail patterns. The fish turned out to be a bright silver rainbow of about 1lb 4oz. The next six casts produced the remainder of my eight-fish limit as I landed two rainbows on my last cast. The limit had taken me thirty-six minutes to achieve once I had removed most of the natural food from my 'swim'. Fifteen minutes later the rise was over. By then I had packed up my gear and was ready for the short walk back to my car.

The floating snails are extremely easy to tie:

Hook: Down-eyed No. 12 and 14 Drennan Sedge.

Tying
Silk: Black
Body: Three strands of peacock-herl, wound tightly over a small triangular-shaped piece of Etherfoam. Tie off, whip-finish and varnish.

Take a small piece of Etherfoam and stick your hook right through it. Trim to a small, triangular shape with a sharp pair of fine scissors, leaving the eye clear of the flat end of the triangle. (See the diagrams.)

Super-glue the ends of the Etherfoam to the hook-shank. Tie on your tying silk and run this over the Etherfoam to the bend of the hook, and tie in the three strands of peacock-herl. Now take the tying-silk back over the body to the eye and tie off.

Wrap the strands of peacock-herl tightly around the body, trying to maintain the general triangular shape, and tie off at the head with a whip finish.

Varnish the resultant 'fly' to give it a shell-like sheen.

Tie up three of each size.

'Swirling' rises are many and varied in nature. They can take the form of a light series of ripples on the water, appearing in ever increasing circles. They can appear as 'great kidney-shaped whorls', as Skues would say, indicating a tremendous sub-surface thrash by a trout chasing a food item. Between these extremes they can appear in a hundred different forms. In general, the greater the displacement of water, the faster the fish has had to move to catch its quarry. This gives us a clue as to what to fish. The gentle rises would indicate the need for a buzzer pupae, fished sub-surface. The more vigorous movements of water would suggest the need for a team of sub-surface sedge pupae, or other faster moving species like the May-fly nymph. These should be fished with a quicker, more darting movement of retrieve than you would employ when fishing buzzer nymphs. Expect 'takes' when the artificials are two to three feet below the surface when fishing to these rises.

Trout feeding on or near the bottom at a depth of six to ten feet will cause a 'flattening' of the water that is readily discernible to the practised eye. When fishing to these rises you need to present your nymphs close to the lake bed and I invariably use a leaded nymph on these occasions. Fish them slowly, or not at all, for best results. I cannot stress enough the importance of static nymph fishing. Nearly all the large, specimen trout I have caught over the years have been taken when I was doing nothing. Nothing except concentrating on my leader, that is.

One memorable afternoon at Pitsford, near Northampton, comes readily to mind. I was fishing in between two pals, and was casting beyond a small weed-bed. There was a good ripple and the wind was straight off our backs. I decided to have some tea, and cast out, as usual. I then began wading back to shore, paying out line as I did so, leaving my team of sedge patterns drifting on the underwater currents. I was just into my second sandwich, my rod on the ground beside me, when I noticed my unchecked reel begin, very slowly, to turn as line pulled off it. Picking up my rod instantly, I hooked and played to the net one of the most beautiful brown-trout I have ever caught. At nearly five pounds, it was the largest brownie taken from that water for many years, and won for me a *Sunday Express* umbrella and a fine bottle of Dry Fly Sherry.

The last rise-form to concern us on the big lake is the splashy wake left by the trout taking food floating on the surface. This can occur during calm or rippled conditions and it heralds the avid feeding that sometimes takes place on spent or waterlogged adult flies. If you see the tell-tale signs of cascading water droplets preceding a series of ever increasing rings, it's always worthwhile trying a dry fly. At one time, dry-fly fishing on big lakes was seldom seen. Today it is a far more common practice and one that the serious trout angler should include in his armoury.

Chapter Five

BOAT FISHING THE BIG LAKES: ANCHORED NYMPH PRESENTATION

I've lost track of the times I've been asked about our methods with fishing the nymph from a boat. That it is successful is witnessed by last year's tally of over four hundred fish for my boat partner and I from Rutland Water, most of them over two pounds in weight, with five glorious trout over five pounds. For us, it is the most pleasurable way of catching reservoir trout. After more than twenty years of trout fishing, the 'take' is what we really fish for these days. The 'fight', and the subsequent 'dispatch' are of secondary importance. The latter often results in complaints about the lack of space in the freezer. Nothing, I feel, gives more excitement than the 'takes' normally experienced when nymph-fishing and it has to be the most relaxed way of trouting imaginable.

There are important rules to observe when boat-fishing in pairs, and casting, strict observance of which may save you or your partner some agony.

Fishing only a few feet apart in a boat, it's inevitable that lines will become tangled unless a strict pattern of casting is maintained. When anchored, especially when the boat is hanging across the wind, the angler sitting in the backward position should always keep his eye on the casting of his downwind partner. When the forward member of the team starts to raise his rod to cast, the fisherman behind him should keep his rod down, and never, in any circumstances, start to cast himself. The line drawings indicate the angles for casting, to which boat-anglers should restrict themselves. Failure to do so will certainly result in tangled lines and may result in injury to your partner; even to yourself.

I was once fishing the 'Boil' at Grafham with my good friend and doctor, Neville Sylveston MBE, that marvellous man who started the Medical and General Practitioners Accident Service (MAGPAS) that has saved the lives of so many road accident victims throughout the Anglia and East Midlands area over the years.

We'd caught quite a few fish, anchored over the turmoil of the water-inlet pipe. There was a fresh wind blowing from the south-west, and we had found the trout to be taking at about thirty-five feet, just

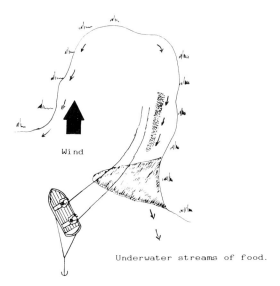

Wind

Underwater streams of food.

Anchor the boat so that you can cast
across the feeding area and retrieve your
nymphs in the same direction as the
underwater current

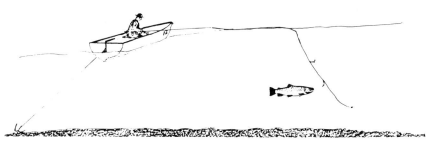

An anchored boat, with nymphs left drifting in underwater currents.
Big fish often find this method irresistible

Four superb Rutland rainbows which fell to anchored nymphs

over the mouth of the pipe. To achieve perfect presentation of our flies, we'd put up ten yards of lead-core shooting head. I was fishing a team of two pheasant-tail nymphs with red thorax's to try to tempt those deep feeding trout, as I knew they were gorging themselves on the millions of large red bloodworms that always seemed to appear when the pumps were turned on. Neville was fishing with a similar line but was using a single lure, a No. 6 long-shanked Jack Frost. This has a red throat and tail and was also taking its share of rainbows.

The boat kept yawing about in the wind and the currents caused by the boil, making casting extremely difficult.

Suddenly Neville yelled, 'You've got me!' and held his hand to his left ear.

'I can't have', I assured him, although I had been casting over his head. 'My flies are twenty-five feet down.' This was the number I'd counted to, since casting out.

'Yes, you have', Neville replied. 'Look!'

I turned my head, to see a large white and red Jack Frost lure sticking right through the lobe of his left ear.

Even after I'd told him what I'd seen, Neville was not convinced until he had recovered sufficient of his line to get it to pull, painfully, on his ear.

I wound in my line and put my rod along the boat seats, then cut the leader, gently, away from the lure with a pair of sharp scissors, which I always carry in my pocket.

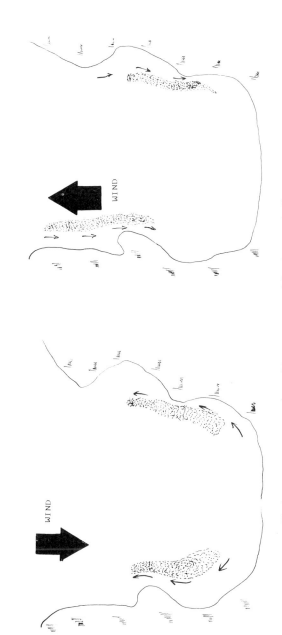

Underwater currents depositing streams of food over shallow areas

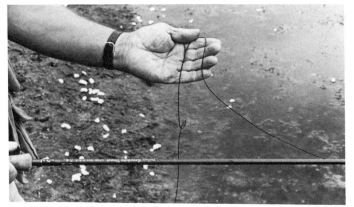

The figure-of-ei
retrieve

1. Gather a loop of fly-line in your palm, as shown

2. Gripping the loop with your last two fingers, pick up another loop with your forefinger

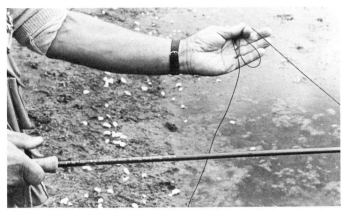

3. Now gather another loop in your palm

4. Grip both loops with the last two fingers and gather another loop with the forefinger

5. Holding the loops with the thumb and forefinger and little fingers alternately, gather more loops with the middle finger

6. The retrieve well under way, eyes concentrating on the end of the leader

Still looking pretty pained, my doctor asked if I had a pair of wire-cutters in my bag. I hadn't. Neither had he.

I lifted the anchor, and with Neville holding a large white hankerchief to his profusely bleeding ear, I started the motor and headed back to the Lodge.

When we landed at the boat harbour the amiable bailiff, Simon, took the doctor to the warden's hut and snipped the hook at the bend, with the biggest pair of callipers I've ever seen. They would have cut through a quarter-inch iron bar!

Anyway it did the trick and the two portions of hook fell away, leaving Neville with a very sore, yet nicely pierced, ear-lobe. After retiring to his car for some first aid – the fishery hadn't a bottle of Dettol in sight – we returned to the boil and later bagged up.

He and I learnt a couple of lessons that day.

First, it's advisable always to have in your tackle bag a sharp pair of small wire-cutters.

Secondly, whenever you're casting in a fresh wind, at anchor, especially with a lead-core line, do wear a hood and sun-glasses to protect your head. I've seen hooks in ears, cheeks and, once, in an eye-lid during my angling career and none of them were any fun for the victim, even if self-inflicted as in Neville's case.

But back to the subject. Boat fishing, at anchor, gives the angler much more scope for nymphing than bank-fishing. Indeed, wind conditions sometimes make nymphing from the bank largely a waste of effort. The most important thing for the aspiring nymph angler to grasp is that, by its very nature, nymphing is an imitative form of fishing (as opposed to attractor fishing) and presentation of the artificial offering, in a natural manner, is absolutely vital to success.

Nymph fishing from an anchored boat is the way we have caught our best and biggest bags of trout. In the 1987 season alone we had over twenty visits to Rutland Water, where we took our full complement of thirty-two fish, employing this method.

Obviously, fish location is of paramount importance if you're going to fish successfully from an anchored boat. There is no substitute for experience and up-to-date local knowledge if you're going to get this right every time. However, there are things you should consider. Food in the big lakes is carried, as in a river, largely by stream. This is especially true of water-borne creatures like nymphs. Try to think where the currents will be running by looking at the contours of the lake shore and taking account of the prevailing wind direction. Wind blowing into a bay, for instance, will almost certainly result in the stream running out of the bay, upwind. Where that current runs from deep water to a shallower area, a natural feeding ground will be created. We like to fish over such areas, where the depth shallows to about eight feet.

Position the boat so that, after casting out your floating fly-line,

Leaded green and brown nymph: two turns of lead wire at the head, lime green ostrich-herl body, pheasant-tail back and tail

This four-pounder fell to a leaded green and brown nymph.
Photo by kind courtesy of *Trout Fisherman Magazine* and Peter Gathercole

the wind-drift will bring your nymphs round *in the same direction as the stream*. If you anchor your boat in the normal way only one of the anglers in the boat will be able to fish correctly. Until we found the answer to this problem we used to change ends about every half an hour. Now we both enjoy sport by tying a length of rope from the bow to the anchor rope or from the stern to the anchor rope, depending on the wind direction. The knot where this rope joins the anchor rope is then slipped down towards the anchor until the boat 'hangs' in such a position that both anglers can obtain the essential 'with the stream' drift of the nymphs.

When you have got this right the takes will usually be spectacular. The fly-line will zip away from you, as the trout takes off with your nymph and all that will be required is a smart lifting of the rod to set the hook. Often even this action is unnecessary, as the resistance of the fly-line does the trick for you. Especially if you fine hone your hooks as I do, before and during the fishing day.

Sometimes, usually in bright conditions, the fish are not quite so suicidal. At these times you may experience 'takes' that seem impossible to 'strike'. A change to a shooting-head instead of the full floater will often bring success. This is because the shooting head offers much less resistance to the taking fish than the full line. If you have to do this, you will find you also need to change the anchorage slightly, to enable the shooting head to fish in the same arc as that achieved by the full line.

My cast usually consists of three flies but in rough conditions I prefer two only. I set them so that the distance between the top dropper and the point nymph is roughly equal to the depth of water covered (eight to ten feet), with about six feet between the end of the fly-line and the top dropper. The usual set-up is with a weighted nymph on the point, a buoyant nymph on the top dropper and a No. 12 pheasant-tail on the middle dropper, when there is one. The buoyancy is achieved using seal-fur or hare's-ear in the thorax dressing. Try to assess how the underwater currents will be flowing, cast out in the direction that will allow for natural presentation, and count the nymphs down. Most of my fish, I have to tell you, I catch when this process of doing nothing is going on. When I do start a retrieve, this usually takes the form of three or four figure-of-eights, then a longish pause before figure-of- eighting again. These pauses are often vital for success and, anyway, they leave the nymphs fishing in the likely area much longer than the continuous retrieves practised by most of the anglers I see.

If I repeatedly get fish taking before the point nymph is down I will shorten the leader length. I also do this if I go too long without a take with the long leader. However, before this latter action I will almost certainly try an unleaded nymph first. Colour can be important but we usually manage to get takes with our 'Green and Brown' nymphs which are tied as follows:

This fine rainbow took a floating deer-hair fry pattern.
Photo by kind courtesy of *Trout Fisherman Magazine* and Peter Gathercole

Hooks: Drennan Wet Fly Nos. 14-8
Body: Pale olive-green ostrich herl over which is tied a tail
and back of cock-pheasant-tail fibres. Weighted at the
head-end with fine lead wire if required. Simple, but
wonderfully effective.

Because you can alter the 'hang' of a boat to get the best of wind
conditions, I seldom find it necessary to change to an intermediate line
to catch. When I do have to resort to this method I use the Masterline

intermediate. I find this line sinks much less than its Wetcel counterpart, which it definitely out-fishes when nymphing.

When the sedge season starts I change to pheasant-tails. I fish a cast of three, with the distance between the top dropper and the point fly roughly the depth of water being covered. My top dropper is normally a No. 14 with a large thorax of hare's ear fibres, to give it buoyancy. The middle dropper, four feet away, would be a No. 12 pheasant-tail with rabbit or coloured seal's fur thorax, and on the point I'd fish a No. 10 pheasant-tail, leaded or unleaded depending on the strength of the wind (and therefore the underwater currents) and the depth at which takes occur. If the fish are taking the middle dropper, for instance, I might change from a leaded point fly to an unleaded one. This would allow both of the bottom nymphs to fish slowly down through the taking area. On the other hand, if the underwater current was strong, I'd keep the leaded point fly on to give stability to the nymphs as they drift along in the stream. For those of you who have been coarse fishermen, it's the equivalent of putting on a heavier float, with a subsequent increase in weight on the cast, when fishing a fast flowing river.

Fishing nymphs that imitate sedges or other large nymphs, like damsels, requires a retrieve slightly modified from that used when copying buzzers. These larger nymphs frequently move up and down in the water in quick darts, emerging from the surface film much faster than their buzzer counterparts. I use inch-long pulls on the line to retrieve these p/ts, stopping every two or three seconds for a similar period to let the nymphs drop attractively down through the water again. The final lift-off before recasting is done with a slow but steady sweep of the rod, just enough to keep the top dropper swimming fairly quickly through the last few feet of surface film. Takes at this point can often be devastating and I have many times been smashed, through lack of concentration, as a trout belted the p/t to prevent its 'escape'.

The sacrificial nymph method can work well from an anchored boat. This method demands a leader with an extra long distance between the middle dropper and the point fly, maybe as much as fifteen feet. This allows the leaded point fly to snag bottom, firmly, so that when the line is tightened slightly the middle and top droppers are being fished in mid-water. The point fly is thus 'sacrificed'. But I have to warn you of the trouble I caused my boat partner, recently, when fishing by this method.

I'd set my leader up with fourteen feet between the middle dropper and the point fly, a heavily leaded version of our Green and Brown Nymph, as we were fishing over about ten to twelve feet of water.

I'd only been fishing a few minutes, when I had a classic static nymph take, where the fly-line picks up slowly and steadily as a fish swims away with the fly in its mouth, having hooked itself. I tightened gently into the fish and the sudden heavy pressure, as line and then

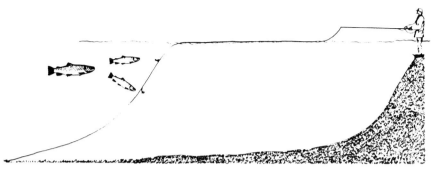

The sacrificial nymph method. Tapping the rod with a finger will impart all the movement necessary to the nymphs, which are anchored by the point fly, to fish in the taking area

backing sailed off my reel, indicated it was another of the South Arm's three-pound-plus overwintered rainbows. It was a full five minutes before I had the fish sufficiently under control to get it somewhere near the boat. Only then did I realise that the trout had picked up the bottom dropper. Now I was in a spot of bother, for, with the top dropper close to the tip of my ten-foot rod, the fish was swimming another twenty feet away!

'We're going to have some trouble now, Pete', I exclaimed. 'The stupid b . . .'s taken the leaded Green and Brown on the point!'

'Hang on, mate. I'll wind in and give you a hand', Pete said, as he started to reel in feverishly.

Then the inevitable happened. His reel suddenly screeched, as line and backing flew off it, and I realised he was into a fish too. As luck would have it Pete's fish was also obviously a good one and, try as he did, his fish seemed obsessed with crossing over to my side of the boat, where my own fish lay, beaten, some ten feet out!

'Careful, Pete!' I called, 'Or we'll lose both of them!'

'I can't help it, mate', he shouted. 'I think I've foul hooked it!'

After what seemed like an eternity, Pete eventually netted his fish and dispatched it. As he had thought, the beautifully conditioned 3lb 12oz rainbow had been hooked, firmly, in the dorsal fin. By this time I was extremely concerned for the hook-hold on my own fish, which had been laying out there for several minutes. Then, just to add to the agony, Pete's hook got caught in the landing net mesh.

'The chap who sold me this said this couldn't happen with this type of netting', Pete moaned. 'I ought to get him to get the blasted hook free!' he swore.

Eventually, of course, he succeeded in freeing his pheasant-tail nymph from the net and asked me to stand on the boat seat and keep my rod as high as possible. With Pete extending the landing net to its fullest extent I was able to manoeuvre the rainbow over the waiting net and our ordeal was over. The whole episode had taken nearly twenty minutes to complete and Pete and I were pretty well exhausted at the end of it. Still, we had two lovely fish to show for our efforts and were able to count our blessings as, later, we each supped a cup of tea!

A spoon inspection of the stomach contents of those two lovely trout clearly indicated the fish were mainly bottom feeding, with lots of snails mixed with the odd large olive buzzer nymph. I shortened my leader so that the leaded Green and Brown nymph on the point would fish just on or slightly off the bottom, and boated five more two-pound-plus rainbows and a three-pound brownie to complete my eight-fish limit. These weighed a creditable 20lb 4oz on the scales in the Fishing Lodge gutting room and looked a picture as they lay in the sink. The South Arm, so often unpredictable, had come up trumps again.

The method is now an everyday part of our nymphing repertoire and is one which has brought its rewards many times during recent seasons. It also seems to pick out the better fish that are around, so don't fish with less than six-and-a-half-pound leaders. I was broken, on the take, last season in July, whilst fishing near the Dead Trees at the bottom of Rutland's South Arm. The fish had clearly taken the middle dropper, a No. 12 Green and Brown nymph and, by the tail-skitting display it made as it took off with the bottom section of leader, it weighed five pounds plus!

One final tip that may help you succeed with the sacrificial nymph method. Pretend, after tightening into the snagged point nymph, that you've got D.T.s, that gentle shaking of the hands that befalls the heavy drinker in the mornings. This seems to impart an irresistible wriggling of the suspended nymphs that often results in a vicious take and, if successful, the capture of a better than average trout. Try it, but don't let your friends see you. They may think you've been at the bottle!

Chapter Six

BOAT FISHING THE BIG LAKES:
DRIFTING NYMPH PRESENTATION

Nymphs, fished from the front of a drifting boat, are sometimes successful as attractors. That is to say, they catch fish even though they are not fished, for most of the time, so that they behave like a real insect. Perhaps you can remember catching a trout on a pheasant-tail, or other nymph, when ripping back line to cast to a rising fish? However, the surest way to be successful with nymphs in front of a drifting boat is to fish them with as natural a presentation as possible.

I, personally, only fish this method when competing in matches that demand international rules, as I much prefer nymph fishing from anchor or bank. Since leaded nymphs are banned from these competitions, I tie my nymphs for this style on heavy Partridge hooks, tied short like a low-water salmon fly. My normal pale olive nymph which we call our 'Green and Brown', with pheasant-tail tail and back, satisfies me for most of the season, although I do use pheasant-tail nymphs, proper, once the sedges start to appear in reasonable numbers. I also tend to fish three flies for this style of angling, and use a twelve-foot carbon rod for floating line fishing and a ten-footer for sunk-line work. My cast would, usually, comprise a No. 10 olive nymph on the point, a No. 12 or 14 of similar pattern on the middle dropper about eight feet away, and an olive buzzer pattern four feet further up the cast. To add to or subtract from the depth I wish the flies to fish, I alter only the leader length *above* the top dropper. I use Drennan Double Strength nylon of 7lb, 6lb or 5lb breaking strain: 7lb in rough, cloudy conditions, 5lb when it is bright and calm.

I use these leaders for floating or sunk-line fishing, depending on the depth of water being covered and/or the surface activity of the fish. If I am in charge of the boat I like to fish over natural feeding sites wherever possible, places where the current flows onto a shallower area. If you can keep the boat on a drift that covers water of a similar depth, say eight to twelve feet, so much the better. In this way, your nymphs will be fishing at more or less the same distance from the lake bed for much of the drift. When this is not possible it may take several drifts over the

Rod held high, a lively trout comes to the net for this loch-styler

same area to 'sound' out the taking depth, with the counting down technique we always use.

The trick is to cast out and take up line in such a way that the drift of the boat is exactly countered by the retrieve. This results in the flies dropping naturally through the water until the final lift of the rod brings them vertically upwards, in a natural manner. When the top dropper appears the rod is dropped slightly to allow the nymphs to 'dangle' for a few seconds. It is at this time that takes often come because, with the rod held high, the nymphs are near the surface and are now moving downwind in the same way as the boat and the natural food in the surface drift. Other times when extra vigilance is often rewarded are the first few seconds after the cast has been made, and during the final retrieve of the cast by the uplift of the rod.

When the cast is first made the nymphs are momentarily in the surface drift and moving, therefore, quite naturally. When the nymphs begin their final ascent, by the uplift of the rod, they come round in a tantalising curve. It is this round-the-bend movement that trout find so irresistible at times.

'Takes' aren't usually so pronounced as they are when nymphing from anchor, probably because the presentation is not as natural, but they are often strikable, even if you feel your reactions are a bit slow, because until the taking fish feels resistance it usually continues to mouth the fly. I certainly find I catch more trout per 'offer' than when luring, though I must admit I find it difficult to concentrate when fishing lures.

Weather conditions can badly affect the fishing of nymphs from the front of a drifting boat. If the wind is anything more than a light breeze, try to slow the boat down as much as possible , especially when fishing over water more than ten feet deep. Move the drogue until the boat is drifting straight down the wind, as any deviation from this straight path can adversely affect presentation. Having got the boat on a nice straight path avoid moving heavy items about in the boat, such as tackle-bags, anchors etc., as this can easily change the drift again.

Restrict yourself to two flies per cast in strong wind conditions, otherwise you may find much of your fishing time is spent getting out of tangles and tying new leaders. In competition fishing this time factor is of the utmost importance. Every minute you spend with your flies out of the water is a minute lost in these time-limit matches. Seconds spent removing tangles, tying on new flies, replacing leaders, motoring to a new drift, eating or drinking, amount to lost time, that can't be replaced during the event.

Pre-match preparation of tackle can save vital minutes during the competition. New leaders, with super-glued droppers, can be tied in readiness and kept on special no-tangle leader spools. Nymphs can, if you wish, be ready tied onto those spare leaders. Anything that will save you time on the day is worth your consideration. Inspect your reels, lines, net and rods for any defects that might cause problems during the competition. Pre-hone the hooks you expect to use. Make yourself a check-list of tackle and accessories, like hook-honer, scissors, Polaroids, etc. It's too late to find something missing after you've left the jetty.

For several days before the competition get the weather forecasts for

A slender, well muscled bar of silver, with a full tail – the unmistakable signs of a big-lake rainbow.
Photo by kind courtesy of *Trout Fisherman Magazine* and Peter Gathercole

Two and a half pounds of typical big-lake rainbow.
Photo by kind courtesy of *Trout Fisherman Magazine* and Peter Gathercole

the area in which you're fishing. Check this with a map of the venue, preferably one showing depth contours if you're not familiar with the water. Where winds have been prevailing for several days in a given direction it should be possible to pin-point, with some certainty, those places where good fish holding spots are likely. This will become a more important consideration now that fisheries are stopping new stockings before match days. It will no longer be the anglers who find a shoal of easy 'stockies' who come off best during the day. Fish location skills will need to be combined with good presentation skills if you want to succeed.

Plan your drifts so that you stick as close to the boat harbour as possible. Unnecessary travelling on the water is a waste of time. Plan drifts that will keep you over similar depths of water for as long as possible, giving you the best opportunity to sort out the taking depth.

When you find out who has been allocated to be your boat partner, find him and tell him, or her, the plans you've made. Try to persuade him to let you stay on the motor all day. The last thing you want is a boat partner who insists on taking you all over the lake every two hours, to fish his pet spot. You've more chance of catching leprosy than of catching a trout with your flies out of the water. Although, I swear, it did happen to me once.

One evening I was fishing on the dam, at Grafham, next to the manager's wife, Mrs Fleming-Jones, a delightful lady and excellent fisher, like her husband, David.

I was fishing at berth 8 – the wall of Grafham has, conveniently, numbers all along it – a swim I always favour in a southerly or south-westerly breeze. The evening had been dull but warm and quite a few fish had been taken by boats anchored sixty or seventy yards out from my station. It all augured well for later and the breeze continued, giving us the advantage of a good ripple.

I'd been fishing with a team of pheasant-tails with a red thorax, the lake bed off this area of the dam having a large population of bloodworm.

My floating line was bowing gently to my right in the ripple and, as it swung round bringing my twenty-foot leader onto the slope of the dam wall, a rod-length out, I had a classic nymph-take. The line zipped up from the end of my rod as a good fish made off with the point pheasant-tail in its scissors.

After a hectic battle, and with arms aching, I finally netted a most beautiful hen-rainbow, with full tail and red fins: a perfect specimen in every way and weighing, I judged, about three and a half pounds. I dispatched it quickly without moving back up the wall and, un-hooking it, threw the flies onto the concrete about a foot above the water level. A spoon inspection showed it to be full of dark, olive-coloured nymphs, a few red bloodworms and a decaying perch-fry of about four inches in length.

I took the trout along thirty yards of the dam, to where Mrs Fleming-Jones and her lady companion were fishing, proudly displaying the lovely fish with both hands.

I was discussing my method of fishing, fly-pattern etc. when I heard a reel scream, and watched, helplessly as my rod started to descend the dam wall towards the lake, line running off my reel at a rate of knots!

I rushed back to my swim just in time to save my rod from disappearing under the water and, slowly, began to make headway against the strong surges the trout was making towards the sludge lagoon.

When I eventually netted it I was amazed. It looked a perfect replica of the rainbow I had just been showing off. They were a pigeon pair and the envy of the small group of anglers who had now joined me to watch me unhook it.

I swear to this day that that fish must have climbed the dam wall to take the pheasant-tail!

Anyway, back to the drifting-boat tactics. If you find a shoal of taking trout, go back through them in short drifts, as often as possible until 'offers' cease. In big competitions, of course, this may be easier said than done. For what usually happens as soon as someone catches is that boats from all over converge on the scene of activity. Try not to get frustrated if this happens. A tense angler is usually a poor one on the day. If you find yourself getting wound up try hard to relax. Do some deep breathing . . . anything that will ease the pressure. Concentrate on the nymphs at the end of your leader to make sure they continue to fish in a natural manner. A relaxed trouter will always out-fish an uptight partner.

If you get no takes using a floating line change to a Hi-Speed Hi-D. Many anglers don't believe you can fish nymphs on this line. I can assure you, you can. Sometimes, when fish are taking food near the lake bed and the drift is such that the floater doesn't allow the nymphs to fish deep enough, the fast-sinker is the only way to overcome the problem. With the Hi-D the skill is in casting, then just keeping in touch with your flies and leader without actually retrieving line until it is close to the lake bed. Then, with a steady retrieve, drawing in line as slowly as possible given the drift of the boat, a trout may be yours. The all-important 'dangle' of the nymphs, rod held high, will allow them to fish, momentarily, with the top-water drift, in a natural, and enticing way.

Every now and then – it happened only twice to me last season – we have the phenomenon of seemingly every trout in the lake rising before us. You need to watch the rises carefully to determine whether the fish are after buzzers, sedges or other large nymphs. Remember, the fish moving slowly from rise to rise will almost certainly be after buzzers.

The fast movers will be chasing the larger nymphs. Often the fish on the buzzer hatch are extremely difficult to tempt. I would try these with a team of suspender buzzers, or Magics, but, I must admit, with not much confidence. I have had some success, when the trout are after sedges and the like, with what I call my pheasant-tail muddler. This fly is tied on a No. 12 nymph hook and is basically a pheasant-tail nymph, tied round the bend, without a tail, with a nice big thorax of deer-hair, trimmed into a small ball at the head of the nymph, about the size of a small pea. I rub Gink into the heads of these nymphs so that they sit in the surface film, and I fish them statically in front of a rise. The result is sometimes electrifying and it pays to keep the rod well up to absorb the smash 'takes' that can ensue when fishing this method. If possible, I like to fish this way with a short line, casting only about fifteen to twenty yards in front of the boat and a yard or two in front of a rising fish; I then wait for a 'take'. If refused, I wait for another rising fish and cast again. The Leeda Ultra floating fly line is ideal for this style, as it floats higher in the surface film than most lines and is, therefore, easier to pick up and re-cast.

I am often asked why I persevere with nymph fishing when others are doing well on lures. The truth is I prefer the more leisurely approach that nymph fishing brings to our sport and am convinced, in my own mind, that nymphing produces the better quality fish, the fry season apart, for most of the trouting year. It's a bit like the difference between the roach caught on maggots to those caught on casters. Anyway, why fish for avidly feeding trout with anything other than a natural food imitation?

Judging by the way they fish on video, some of our most successful international trout fishermen would not agree with the foregoing paragraphs; they seemingly strip their flies back to them, some of them nymphs. My analysis of their method is that they strip an attractor across the surface to interest any passing fish and then fish the flies and nymphs quite naturally for a moment or two, with rod held high, before recasting. Would it not be better, I ask myself, if they tried to fish the nymphs naturally throughout the retrieve. Although I haven't had the pleasure of fishing with ex world champion, Brian Leadbetter, I believe his style more closely follows my own and is achieving a natural presentation throughout.

Some anglers have, I know, tried nymph-fishing and been unsuccessful. They have turned back to their dog-knobblers and other offerings, and who can blame them? They almost invariably went wrong by fishing their nymphs too fast. Many years ago now, I was fishing the north shore at Grafham and finding the going hard, despite the fact that the angler next to me had four nice fish on the bank, and was clearly fishing the nymph. Eventually he came up to me and asked me to try fishing my nymphs at a *quarter* of the speed I had been fishing them. Since

I was using a figure-of-eight retrieve at the time, this advice seemed extraordinary, but I followed it none the less. I cast out my floating line, with two of my own No. 12 buzzer-nymphs and the No. 10 dark-olive nymph, with green thorax, that my benefactor had given me. Within two minutes I had a three-pound rainbow nearly pull the rod out of my hand during one of the periods of 'no retrieve' that his method demanded. I suppose I have caught several thousand trout since, when 'doing nothing', so to speak, and it has gained me a reputation for being the luckiest angler around. Anyway, that helpful angler, who set me on the right road from that memorable day, was the great Cyril Inwood – arguably the best nymph-fisherman ever.

Clearly, in a drifting boat it becomes more difficult to 'do nothing' for more than a second or two because the boat is always moving towards your line and would eventually drift over it. However, I believe you should arrest your retrieve every now and then to let the nymphs drop naturally through the water, if only for the briefest of periods.

If I get no 'offers' using a floating line or Hi-D over areas I expect to hold fish, I change to a Wetcel 2. On the face of it this may seem a strange way to operate. Perhaps, you think it best to try the Wetcel 2 before the Hi-D. I have found, though, that most of the time either the floater or the Hi-D will work for me. It's just occasionally that the medium sinker provides the right answer for the day. Cast out with a team of two or three nymphs, spaced evenly along the last twelve feet of an eighteen foot leader. Retrieve just enough to keep in touch with your line as the boat drifts downwind. 'Takes' seldom come soon after you have cast with this line. Much more frequently the trout will snatch at your offering from the depths under your rod-top, just as you start to lift the rod to start the nymphs on their upward path. Make this final ascent fairly quick until the top nymph appears on the surface. Then let the rod-tip drop, momentarily. This will allow the nymphs to descend, naturally, for a few inches, before rising up again. In my experience this is the time when absolute vigilance is essential. Most 'offers' happen at this point and a quick tightening of the line is usually necessary to set the hook. Unlike what happens when fishing at anchor, fish seldom seem to hook themselves when taking nymphs fished from in front of a drifting boat.

Chapter Seven

BOAT FISHING THE BIG LAKES:
THE NORTHAMPTON STYLE

In this chapter I want to describe our methods of presentation whilst fishing in the Northampton style, or 'On the Rudder', as it is more commonly called. There always appears to be an air of mystery surrounding this technique, yet its execution is simplicity itself. We employ this method of fishing by pointing the boat straight down the wind and keeping it, more or less, in this position throughout the drift, by manipulating a rudder attached to the stern. A couple of simple devices, to allow the oars to be trailed on each side of the boat, reduce the amount of work necessary to keep the bows downwind. They can also be used to adjust the angle of the drift from time to time, allowing us to zig-zag across the water, to turn the boat sideways when a fish is being played, and to turn it back downwind as soon as possible after a trout has been boated.

When a boat is drifting in this manner, point first and downwind, its rate of progress is much faster than that of a boat drifting sideways on to the wind. Naturally, the stronger the wind, the faster the boat will travel. This style enables you to cover an enormous area of water during a day, which undoubtedly contributes to its considerable success as a method of catching trout. However, with this style of fishing, as with all the others I have described in other chapters, the correct presentation of the lures is the

key factor for regular success. I say lures because the Northampton style lends itself best to the imitation of a small fish. Indeed, if you see some of the four- and five-inch 'flies' which some anglers use, you'll see that each one's idea of 'small' is not the same. So, remembering those basic rules of fly presentation, that is getting your artificial to resemble the natural at the correct taking depth, let's consider the problems that face us when contemplating fishing in this way.

Clearly, when the boat is drifting so quickly downwind, a line cast out sideways from the boat will speedily straighten out behind the stern, even if no retrieve is made. In this process of straightening out, the line, leader and lure swing round in a semicircle: just the 'round the bend' method of retrieval that so often proves irresistible to a taking trout. The line drawings demonstrate that we can enhance or reduce this swinging

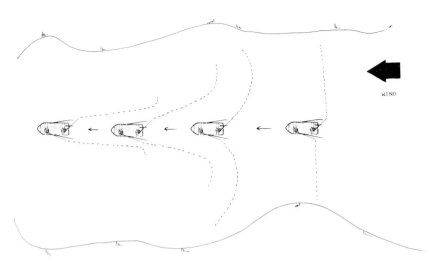

Large areas of water can be covered when employing the Northampton
style. Note the ruddering retrieve pattern, as the boat drifts quickly,
point first, downwind. The angler in the bows retrieves immediately after
casting. The one on the rudder simply allows the drifting boat to bring his
lure round in an arc. Both methods work well

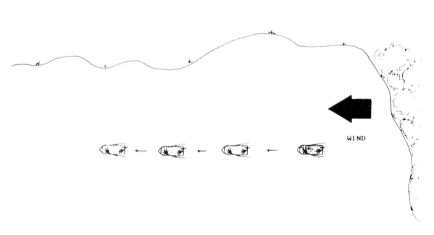

In a big wind, choose a drift protected by trees or high ground, and rudder
along a shoreline wherever possible

effect on the lure, by paying out or retrieving line as the case may be. Also, at the end of the retrieve the artificial will be lifted into the top layer of water, which is moving with and at about the same speed as the boat. Therefore, if we arrest the retrieve at this point and allow the lure to drag along behind the boat for a short while, it will resemble a small dead fry, drifting with the wind.

Sounds good, so far, but what about the correct depth? Here we have quite a problem. Because of the vast area of water being covered, and the fact that during the drift we will not always be over taking fish, we have to devise a systematic method of searching for the right depth, in order to be sure of ultimate success. As the depth of water over which we will be drifting varies so much, lines presenting a lure just off the bottom in one area may snag over others, or be ten feet or more above the lake bed as the drift progresses. This further complicates our attempts to achieve perfect presentation.

On setting out for a day's fishing 'on the rudder', the first consideration is the position of the anglers in the boat. Sidecasting, as this method demands, is, for two right- or left-handed anglers, different from sidecasting for boat-partners of opposite casting actions. Always man the boat in the way that best reduces casting hazards. I once had a long-shank 6 lure stuck in my wrist. It was not a thoroughly enjoyable experience, and it could just as easily have been my eye! In a strong wind, the angler at the stern will not be able to cast safely and will have to make do by paying line out behind the boat before retrieving it. In these conditions it is gentlemanly to change places every couple of hours, because the fisherman in the bows, casting sideways from the boat, will be presenting his lures in the best possible way, and usually catching more trout than his partner.

A check on the weather forecast before your fishing trip will arm you with vital information for a successful day. Plan your day around the forecast. If the wind is going to freshen or change direction during the day, you should take this into account when deciding over which areas to fish. If you're fishing a lake for the first time, try to get hold of a map, showing depth of water contours. Considering the wind direction, plan your drifts so that, as far as possible, you travel over water of fairly constant depth. Nothing is worse, when trying to fish close to the bottom, than snagging up on every other cast. You spend more time cleaning your lure of weed than actually fishing. If the wind is forecast to freshen to strong later in the day, plan your afternoon drifts where you're likely to find some shelter. As I mentioned earlier, in strong winds it's at best dangerous, and at worse impossible, for the angler in the stern to cast. Finally, be sure to have adequate waterproofs with you. Even if it isn't going to rain, travelling up wind on a big lake almost always results in heavy spray drenching anglers and tackle alike. In my Shakespeare box everything stays dry. If you don't possess one, wrap your tackle in a

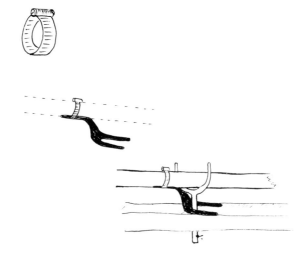

A simple device for trailing the oars
whilst fishing the Northampton style

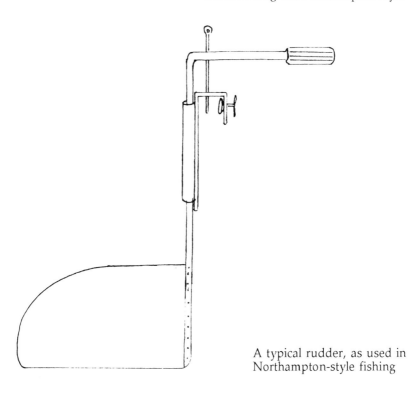

A typical rudder, as used in
Northampton-style fishing

large plastic bag, and wear your Barbour, over-trousers and wellies. A wet, cold fisherman has a job concentrating on the foremost matter of catching trout.

All these things done, you're off to your first drift. Always start that drift from a position that you can precisely find again, if necessary. Lake trout, particularly the rainbows, shoal up for most of the season. If you find taking fish during a drift, you need to be able to find the exact spot again. Twenty- five yards to either side may not be close enough to continue catching.

Now is the time to decide which lines to use. You should each choose a different one. If it's April/May or Sept./Oct. use a ten-yard lead-core shooting head on one rod and a Wetcel High-speed Hi-D on the other. Remember you need a specialised rod to cast a lead-core. It's also a good idea to each fish with a different colour lure to start with. Early and late season use black and white as the alternatives. In midsummer use Canadian lead-impregnated and Wetcel 2 lines to start. At this time of year white or orange lures are favourite. A fifteen foot cast of at least 7lb Drennan Double Strength leader should suffice.

Turning into your first run, point the boat down the wind, cut the engine, let down the rudder and drop the blades of the anchored oars over the side. Now you can begin casting. To do so, or to start paying out line, with the engine running is illegal and cheating.

Cast out, sideways from the boat, and start your retrieve, straight-away, trying to imitate the movements of a small, wounded fish. Whilst you are doing this your line will begin to straighten behind the boat, coming round in a curve as it does so. During the final moments of the retrieve your lure will be travelling in, or close to, the surface. Let it hang for a few seconds before lift-off. This will it resemble a dead fry, floating in the top layer of water and moving with the current.

At the next cast, count to five before repeating the retrieve pattern, and count down each cast by another five until your line straightens behind the boat before retrieval, or you snag bottom, whichever is the earlier. Then start the process over again. If you get an offer, remember the line used and the count. Remember also, and most importantly, the exact location of the take. Both boat partners now change to the winning combination of line and lure and you motor upwind, well away from your line of drift, to put the boat over the mark where the take occurred. You both now cast and count to the number noted and, with luck, you will each have an offer when the boat passes over the right area.

If the first drift proved unsuccessful, try another, from the same starting point, each using a new line, one coming up in the water, the other going deeper. If this doesn't work, start a new drift using the original selection of lines and repeat this systematic and disciplined searching technique until you contact fish again. Then both will repeatedly adopt the successful method over the 'taking' area until offers stop. In early season, when trout are shoaled up in large numbers, it is not uncommon for a boat to 'limit' over quite a small area of water once the fish have been found and the taking depth has been established.

If you see evidence of fish moving on the surface, or that 'flattening' of the water that indicates trout are feeding just a couple of feet down, don't be afraid to change to a floater or intermediate line, if you want to continue to work 'on the rudder'. Using these lines you would, naturally, start retrieving as soon as you had cast out, thus keeping the lure well up in the water.

It is possible to use a drogue in conjunction with a rudder. This would have the effect of slowing the drift and might be used in a very strong wind. The drogue should be tied to a point on the middle of the stern. I must admit, however, that I never use this method, mainly because I don't like the idea of hooking a trout at the back of the boat and then having to worry about it getting snagged up in the drogue. If I want to slow the boat in a high wind, I try to drift over water that is sheltered by high land or trees.

If the wind drops, so that only a light ripple brushes the surface, and the fish are clearly showing on top, try a team of three flies, or even nymphs, on a floater. These, cast sideways Northampton style, often produce a take as the drifting boat brings the line and leader round in an arc.

One other productive way of employing this method in a very light ripple, when fish are showing occasionally near the surface, is to fish a buoyant lure, such as a Muddler. This should be fished from a floater, high in the water. Cast sideways, as usual, and pay out the whole of your fly-line. As the line starts to straighten behind the boat, the lure will come round in a slow enticing arc. The sight of a five-pound rainbow chasing it round the bend is guaranteed to make your heart skip a beat or two!

Never, ever be tempted to lay your rod down on a boat seat with the line over the back of the drifting boat.

A couple of my pals were out ruddering one day at Grafham, during the time when Hayden Jones was in charge. At this time the method and the 'wagglers' they were using were strictly taboo, and they were undoubtedly cheating. Perhaps you will agree that there is a moral attached to this story.

Any way, one of the guilty parties decided to light up a cigarette and laid his rod on the seat behind him, in order to cup his hands round his lighter. He dropped the reel, so that it hung down over the seat's edge with the top section of the rod laid over the stern of the boat. He'd done it many times before and saw no reason for it to be in any way unsafe.

There was a big wind on the lake that day and the point-down boat was travelling at a fair rate of knots. Before the chap with the Benson and Hedges in his hand could reach his rod, the reel had jumped up over the seat ledge and the whole caboodle had flown over the back of the boat, reel screaming, with a trout firmly secured to the business end of the leader.

As the boat drifted further and further away from the now upturned rod, the latter began to disappear beneath the waves like a giant stick-float on the Trent. Despite the desperate efforts they made to turn the boat to recover the rod, line and fish, they were too late. When they got in the general direction of the disappearing rod, there was no trace of it. Desperate to recover the valuable property, the two anglers tried, for two hours, to grapple the line up with heavy lures on sinking lines: all to no avail.

'Whatever sort of fish would do something like that?' the one enquired of the other.

'Probably a double-figure rainbow', his mate replied.

'What a bastard!' the rodless one returned. 'And I've only just had a claim on my insurance for a broken rod.'

'They'll probably stop your policy', the other bantered.

'Hope you're not right', came the miserable reply.

Anyway, I think the two repented their sins, because they stopped fishing the Northampton style and started to fish off the front of the boat, loch style, for the rest of the day.

The gods certainly seemed to approve, because at 3 o'clock that afternoon, when they were drifting over some water quite close to where the rod had disappeared, the chap who lost it caught a snag with his Hi-Speed Hi-D. Yes, you've guessed it. When he pulled in his line, there, firmly caught in the bend of his lure, was his green Wetcel 2 line, with rod, reel and fish still attached. By this time the fish was pretty lifeless, but the rod, line and reel were still in good shape, if a little muddy.

The fish weighed exactly 2lb 7oz which shows how wrong estimates of lost fish can be, and gives substance to the theory that all fishermen are dreamers.

However, it does show how easy it is to lose valuable tackle, so be warned.

'Ruddering' is condemned by some as being unethical. Personally, I think that's a nonsense, unless it is banned on a water. It can be a rather boring method of fishing, and it's not my favourite way of catching trout. But witness, as I frequently do, the thirty-pound-plus limits produced in this way, lying on the gutting room tables at Rutland Water most weeks of the season, and you'll realise it's an exceptionally productive method, when applied by experts: one certainly worth having in your armoury.

Chapter Eight

FLIES TO ASSIST PRESENTATION
AND CATCH FISH

You may have gathered from previous chapters that I regard the method of presentation and depth at which artificials are fished as being more important than the flies, nymphs or lures used. However, that doesn't mean I don't pay much attention to the imitations I employ. On the contrary, I tie my flies to assist presentation. The materials and hook patterns used are selected depending on the depth I want the flies to fish. I also try to give my artificials an authenticity, to make them as realistic as possible. Here I undoubtedly fail. One of my best fishing pals calls them 'sh..' flies and seldom accepts one, if offered. Plenty of other anglers have also looked in my fly-box with disdain. I care not. I've been catching trout on them for well over twenty years and confidently expect to continue to do so for many seasons more, I hope. Don't let this put you off buying the best tied flies you can afford. If that gives you confidence, so be it. On the other hand, if what I have just said persuades you to have a go at tying your own, go to it. Catching fish on your own flies is satisfying and the hours spent at the tying-vice are peaceful and relaxing.

Every year I create or copy several new patterns and my fly collection must run into thousands. Yet, if I were forced to discipline myself to fish a dozen different patterns only, I would be happy to oblige. Very rare would be the occasion when I'd have to revert to another choice of fly, nymph or lure, in order to catch.

Here, then, are the twelve artificials, I'd choose.

LURES

1. *Waggler*

As you can see from the photograph this lure is really fish-like in appearance. Its plastic tail, bought from Flexi-tail, and available in white, black, orange and other colours, 'waggles' attractively as it is retrieved. Keep movements to short, sharp darts, or slow but continuous, hand-

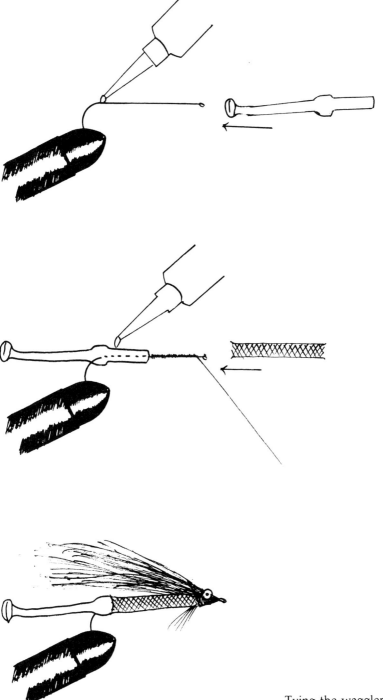

Tying the waggler

over-hand, retrieval. The wing of white, black or orange marabou gives movement to the lure when retrieval is stopped and as it sinks down. The sparkling flashabou, from Lureflash Products, makes it shimmer in the light, much as small fish do when they twist and turn in the water. The body-tube and optic-eyes, from the same company, simply adds to the authenticity.

Tie the lures as follows.

Hook: Long-shank No. 10 or 6 depending on Flexi-tail size (large or mini-tail).

Tying silk: Black. First cover the hook shank with tying silk and tie off.

Tail: Slip the Flexi-tail over the hook shank and glue in position with a dab or two of super-glue.

Body: Cut a piece of body tube to fit over the 'body' part of the Flexi-tail to just short of the eye of the hook. Fix at each end with super-glue.

It will assist you get a good join if, after you have applied the body tube to the glued area of the Flexi-tail, you whip a couple of winds of tying silk over the tube, at the join, and hold it there for a few seconds.

The tube at the eye end of the hook shank can be fixed with tying silk.

Wing: Tie in a thin layer of flashabou. Top this with a thicker layer of marabou.

Head: Build up a head to match the thickness the body, with black tying thread. Tie off with a whip finish and varnish.

When dry, fix eyes on each side of the head with super-glue.

Throat hackle: Optional red or orange dyed cock-hackle.

Tie up three of each size in various blends of colour.

Plain white wing, white tail and silver body. White and orange wing, white tail and silver body. White and red wing, white tail and silver body. The same again, using pearly bodies.

Plain black wing, black tail and silver body. Black and red wing, black tail and silver body. The same again with a gold body.

Plain orange wing, orange tail and pearly body. White on orange wing, orange tail and pearly body and finally a plain white wing, orange tail and pearly body.

This will give you a fine selection of wagglers, which will cater for every condition. Fish the large sizes at all times except when the needle fry are showing round the jetties. When this occurs the smaller waggies really score.

Tying the leach lure

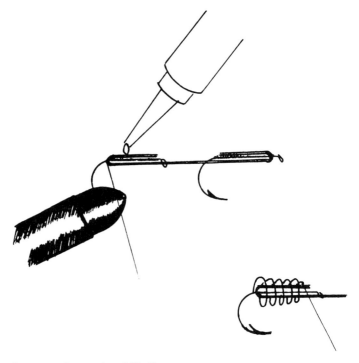

Creating a tandem using 30lb Stren

2. Marabou 'Leaches'

This bushy lure is tied with a heavy, double marabou wing for a certain amount of buoyancy and an incredible amount of movement when fished, as it should be, very slowly during the early or late fishing season.

Tie them simply, as follows.

Hook: Long-shank No. 10.
Tying silk: Black or white to match.
Body: Black or white plain chenille.
Wing: Two large tufts of black or white marabou, one tuft tied about a third of the way up the hook shank from the bend, the other just behind the eye.
Head: Black or white tying silk to match, whip-finished and varnished.

Tie three of each colour. I cannot stress too much how slowly this lure has to be fished for best results. Inch long, slow pulls are all that are needed. Use an intermediate from the bank on the first day, with one of these on a twelve-foot leader of 6lb Drennan Double Strength and be confident of catching, if you've chosen your location well. Fish the black one if it's overcast, the white one in sunlight.

3. *Tandem Lure*

This traditional tandem lure is one that I have great faith in at the back-end of the year, when the fish-fry are getting larger. I have caught many of my five-pound-plus fish on this fly and favour the white and orange particularly where large brownies are expected.

> *Hooks*:   Two long-shank No. 8s. These are tied and super-glued together using 30lb nylon, as shown in the diagram.
> *Tying silk*: Black.
> *Tails*:   Orange cock-hackle fibres tied from both hook bends.
> *Bodies*: Plain black or white chenille.
> *Rib*:   Fine silver wire.
> *Wings*:   Light bunch of black or white marabou over which is tied a thin layer of grey squirrel-tail. Tie the wings on both hooks.
> *Throat hackle*: Orange cock-hackle fibres tied on the
> under-side of each hook at the eye.

Tie up three of each colour. This lure can be fished with foot-long darting movements or by continuously retrieving, hand over hand.

4. *Floating Fry*

This lure really comes into its own when the trout start moving in among the weed-beds to mop up fish-fry. Typically the cannibals strike into a shoal of fry, their mouths chomping at everything in sight. Then they turn and clear up the stragglers – those fry that are dead or injured. It is one of these dead or injured fry that this lure is designed to imitate, tied with white deer-hair, with a tuft of red deer-hair to represent bloody gills. As you can see from the photograph, it is tied in such a way that the body lies on its side with the hook protruding underneath.

Tie this lure as follows.

> *Hook*:   Long-shank Nos. 4, 6 and 8.
> *Tying silk*: White.
> *Body*:   White deer-hair, with a couple of tufts of red deer-hair where the gills would be. Tie the deer hair in tight tufts, starting at the bend by holding the hair by its ends and winding the tying silk across the middle of the hair, against the hook shank. This will cause the two ends of the deer hair to stick upwards. Keep the tied tufts tight as you progress along the hook to the eye. Tie off with a whip finish and varnish.

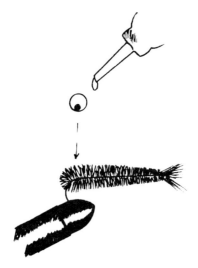

The deer-hair fry is shaped like a small fish. Note the hook at the head end. Optic eyes, from Lureflash Ltd, are super-glued on for added authenticity

Now comes the difficult part. Taking a pair of sharp, point-nosed scissors, trim the deer hair until you have the shape of a small fish with the head at the hook end of the shank. This is important.

Many years ago now, when I was seven or eight and just at the start of World War II, I used to spend part of my summer holidays with an old uncle who lived in a little cottage by the Great Ouse river at St Ives, in Huntingdonshire, as it was then called.

My Uncle George was an excellent eel fisher, perhaps the best there has ever been, and sent large numbers of these slimy creatures to Billingsgate every day during the summer. I had the job, an idyllic one for a young boy, of catching the many gudgeon he needed to bait his traps and night-lines. Later during the day I would sit on an up-turned, galvanised bucket, with a cushion on top, carefully threading the fine line, tied to long hooks, through the gudgeon. These were later tied to long night-lines with, perhaps, as many as twenty baits to each long-line.

Uncle always insisted that I thread the baiting needle from the gills to the vent, leaving the bend and barb of the hook at the head end of the gudgeon. 'Eels and all predatory fish,' he told me, 'take their prey head-first.' It's a lesson I never forgot and when I came to tie my first floating fry it seemed the logical way to tie these too.

I have fond memories of those summer holidays, sitting on the steps of the quay at St Ives, next to the historic bridge, my bread-paste ball covered by a damp cloth to keep it moist, and my small rod and reel the envy of some of my young friends who only had lines tied to hazel twigs with which to fish. We put all the gudgeon we caught into a bucket of water to keep them fresh and put all the roach and dace back. Eels preferred gudgeon, Uncle George said.

Then as dusk fell we'd get into his flat-bottomed punt, loaded with eel-traps and baited lines, and pole quietly up-river to lay those same traps and lines in the special places along the Ouse and its dreamy backwaters that only Uncle George seemed to be able to spot.

Next morning we'd be back again to retrieve them – at first light, before the poachers could lay their hands on them, putting up the herons and ducks as we glided across the grey, mist-shrouded water. Our work done, we'd paddle home to his little riverside cottage, where my kind Auntie Mabel would be cooking an aromatic breakfast of eggs, bacon and fried bread. But that's another story.

Finish off the lure with two optic-eyes, super-glued to each side of the head. Tie up three of each size.

NYMPHS

1. *Green and Brown (Olive) Nymph*

This fly has caught me thousands of trout and is the nymph I most commonly use. Tying it is simplicity itself but it is vital to get the body colour just right. The only thing I can tell you is that Veniards sell this ostrich herl and it is a yellowy-olive colour. Since the packets have no identification on them, that's the best I can do. Fish it on the point, below two ordinary buzzer nymphs. I tie it unleaded or with two or four turns of lead wire beneath the head, depending on hook size (see below). For best effect, fish this pattern very, very slowly, or not at all.

Tie the nymphs as follows.

Hook: Sizes 8, 10, 12 and 14 Partridge Grey Shadow Captain Hamilton Wets.

Tying silk: Black. Starting at the eye, line the shank to the bend, with one layer of tying silk.

Body: Tie in three strands of yellowy-olive ostrich herl at the bend and tie in five strands of cock-pheasant fibre, also at the bend, with about a third of an inch of the pointed pheasant-tail fibres protruding as a tail. Wrap the ostrich herl round the hook shank and tie off at the eye. Now bring the rest of the pheasant-tail fibres over the top of the body to form a back and tie off at the eye. Make a small head of tying silk, whip-finish and varnish.

Tie up three of each size unleaded and three of each size leaded. Use four turns of fine lead wire beneath the heads of the Nos. 8 and 10 and two turns under the heads of the Nos. 12 and 14. Although a very simple nymph to tie, if I were allowed to use only one fly pattern, this would be the one. In the water its slim outline looks very realistic.

I also tie this pattern with red, black and orange ostrich herl, leaded and unleaded as above. Fish the black nymph in very poor light, the orange when green algae are in the water, and the red nymph when bloodworms abound.

3. Black, Grey and Green Buzzer Nymphs

I usually fish these nymphs on the top or middle droppers. I keep them lightweight, so that they are presented to the trout in the top two or three feet of water. When inched in very slowly, with regular pauses, they rise and fall very much as a natural buzzer nymph would behave.

Tie them as follows.

Hook: Nos. 12, 14 and 16 Drennan Midge.
Tying silk: Fine black, grey or light green.
Body: The lightest possible covering of appropriate tying silk after tying in a tiny tuft of white rabbit fur and a piece of very fine silver wire well round the bend.
Rib: Very fine silver wire wrapped round the body in the opposite direction to the tying silk, creating segments every sixteenth of an inch to just below the eye.
Thorax: A couple of turns of ostrich herl. Black for the black bodies, dark green for the grey bodies and light brown for the green bodies.
Head: Tied the same colour as the bodies with a light tuft of white rabbit fur over the eye. Whip-finish and varnish.

Tie three of each size and colour.

Tie some others in the form of suspender-buzzers.

These are tied exactly as the black, grey and green buzzer nymphs, above, except that in place of the small tuft of white rabbit fur at the eye, a tiny white polystyrene ball, encased in a small piece of old nylon stocking, is tied in. This enables the nymphs to sit, suspended, in the surface film. They should be fished with a static presentation, a light tapping on the rod butt with a finger giving them the only movement they need.

Tie three of each size and colour.

4. Magics   (see p. 33, 34)

Tie three of each of these in the hook sizes shown.

I believe these patterns are taken for emergent buzzers, and, as such, they should be fished in or very near the surface. The large, more buoyant, thorax and positioning of the wings make the flies sit

White and Orange Tandem Lure . Black Leach
Deer-hair Fry . Pearly Invicta . White Invicta
Green and Brown Nymph . Mallard and Claret . Buzzer Nymphs (3)
Mini and Maxi Wagglers

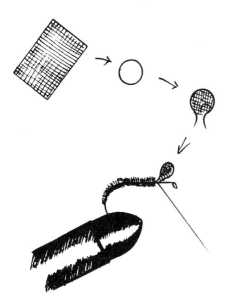

Tying the suspender buzzer nymph

attractively in the water, always sinking hook-bend first when retrieval is arrested. They aren't much to look at, and I have had them refused by anglers when I've offered one to them, but I wish I had a pound for every fish they've caught me and my pals over the years.

SEDGES

The following are three sedge patterns I would hate to be without during July and August.

1. *Silver Invicta*

I use the standard dressing for this fly and tie it in sizes 10, 12 and 14 on Partridge Grey Shadow Captain Hamilton, wet-fly hooks. I also tie a variant with, instead of the silver lurex body, a pearly lurex from Lurefast Products. This fly has fished well for me in recent seasons and is worth a try on some of the harder fished waters where the trout have seen hundreds of traditional Silver Invictas. Fished loch-style, remember the fish chasing sedges will be moving at speed. If you cast to a rising fish, try to judge its direction of travel and cast well in front of its last position, before retrieving in short, sharp pulls of about six inches.

Tie three of each size in each variant.

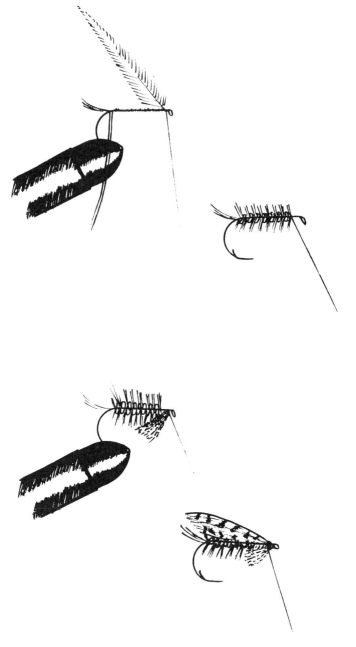

Tying the Silver Invicta

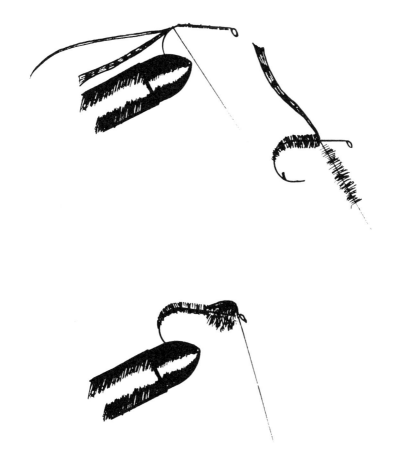

The pheasant-tail sedge imitation

2. *Standard Invicta*

I again use the standard dressing, in sizes 10, 12 and 14 and tie a variant with a white, floss-silk body in sizes 14 and 16. This has out-fished the standard pattern for me during the last few seasons. Presentation is as its silver counterpart.

Tie three of each size in each variant.

3. *Mallard and Claret*

This is my favourite sedge pattern as dusk falls. Tied traditionally in

The standard pheasant-tail

sizes 8, 10 and 12 and fished as the Invictas, I have caught some magic brownies on this fly over the years.

Tie three of each size.

PHEASANT TAILS

1. *Sedge Pupae*

Once sedges start to appear in any numbers, or when rise forms suggest that trout are taking sedges, I put one of these pheasant tails on my top dropper. Tied with a hare's-ear thorax, for added buoyancy, this fly has probably caught me more three-pound-plus fish than any other single pattern.

Tie it as follows.

> *Hook*:   Drennan Midge Nos. 10 and 12.
> *Tying silk*: Black.
> *Body*:   Cock-pheasant fibres, tied in round the bend and
>   wrapped round the shank to within a quarter of an
>   inch of the eye, then tied off and left to form the thorax
>   cover.
> *Rib*:   Fine copper wire tied to make segments along the body.
> *Thorax*: Make a fairly thick thorax of dubbed hare's-ear. Pull
>   over the cock-pheasant fibres towards the eye and tie
>   off to create a small head. Whip-finish and varnish.

Fish close to the surface and retrieve with fast figure-of-eights, pausing now and then to allow the nymph to sink slowly for a second or two.

Tie three of each size.

2. *Pheasant Tail Nymph*

This fly can represent many of the trout's natural food forms, from a

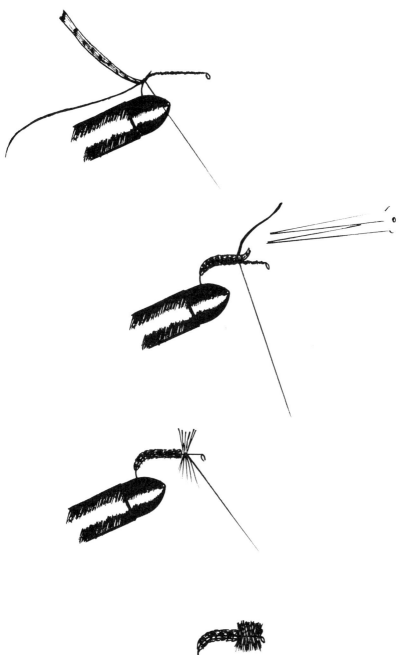

Tying the pheasant-tail muddler

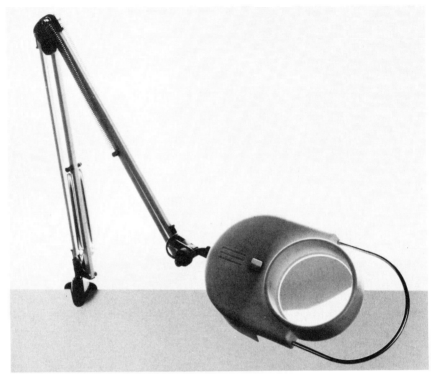

The Anglepoise magnifying lamp, a *must* for fly tying

caddis larva to a small fish-fry. I tie them all with tails from the tips of cock-pheasant tail fibres (about four or five fibres) and with thorax's of rabbit-fur (grey), amber, red, green or brown seal's fur or a substitute. I use the following hooks: long-shank Nos. 6, 8, 10 and 12; Mustad 9672.

Tie three of each size and colour in leaded (use four turns of lead-wire for sizes 6 and 8 and two turns for the smaller sizes) and unleaded form.

Fish them as you would expect the natural you are imitating to behave. The leaded No. 8 make excellent anchors for the sacrificial nymph technique.

The pheasant-tail muddlers I've mentioned in an earlier chapter are sometimes really productive when fished as you would a suspender buzzer. Some of my match-fishing friends also tell me they are excellent as 'bob' flies, making an attractive wake as they cut through the water like skitting sedges. They say that in July and August they sometimes outfish the more common 'bobs', like the Soldier Palmer and the Grenadier.

There are my twelve selections. If you've tied them in the numbers I've suggested you'll have a collection of over four hundred patterns. Replace any you lose or lend and any that get so worn they no longer catch. Hone them to a fine sharpness before use and keep them as dry as possible. They should then give you season after season of good service.

Since writing this chapter I've come across the most useful aid to good fly-tying imaginable. It's a magnifying lamp. Owning one of these will bring a new dimension to your hobby, making it easy to enhance your work up to professional standards. The first pattern I tied, using this new device, I showed to the pal who treats my flies with such disdain. He couldn't believe I'd tied it. Then I showed him the magnifying lamp, and he was convinced. Even size 16 buzzer nymphs appear lure size with this fantastic tool. The company manufacturing the lamp is: Anglepoise Lighting, Unit 51, Enfield Industrial Estate, Redditch, Worcs. B97 6DR. Tel: (0527) 63771.

In fact they make two models. The 8807 is their luxury model. It is splendidly designed and manufactured for those of you who want the best. The 87V07 will be quite adequate for the less fastidious. Its magnification is similar to the 8807's and it offers excellent value. I thoroughly recommend both products.

Chapter Nine

SALMON FEVER

At least once a year, I get what can best be described as an attack of salmon fever.

This all started, several years ago now, when a kind brother-in-law invited me to fish on a private stretch of the River Wye, below Monmouth, in which he owned a partnership. It was April and when I arrived at the fishery, the Wye Valley was basking in the lush green highlights of spring, as the sun shone from a blue, cloudless sky. The birds were in full song and the glistening river tumbled through its boulder-strewn path to the sea. I felt so at peace with my surroundings that, for once, the fishing seemed of secondary importance.

I had been briefed beforehand on the etiquette required of the salmon fisher, and was mindful that the reservoir tactic of getting into a prime fishing position, and staying there, was definitely a non-starter! On the salmon 'beat', not only do you share the water completely, but it is also customary to cast, retrieve and move a pace or two down each pool as you fish. Staying put in one likely spot is most definitely a practice that could put an end to any further invitations you might expect!

At the impressively large fishing hut at the entrance to the fishery, I met the other rods sharing the four and a half miles of fishing that comprised the 'beat'. Listening, politely, to the conversation, it was clear I was in the presence of some very experienced salmon fishers. Indeed, my mouth watered as they recalled recent catches from fisheries as far afield as Alaska and Mongolia. These anglers obviously moved in circles way beyond anything to which my salary would stretch.

I studied them closely as they continued to gossip. Two were tall and well-built: one I judged to be in his mid-thirties, the other a grey-haired chap of more mature years. Their hands were large and rough-skinned and I guessed they were farmers. The third, the one I subsequently learned would be sharing my part of the beat, was a small, thin-featured man, who looked quite out of place in that great outdoors. I found out, later, that he was an accountant in the City and only found time to leave his office about three days a year. Two of them he spent salmon fishing.

After some discussion, the rota for the day's fishing was agreed and I

The author fishing a fly-only pool on the Association Water at Grantown-on-Spey

was introduced to the water warden, who was to act as my 'ghillie', or adviser, during the day.

I learned from the warden that the river was really too high for fly fishing and that my best chance of a fish was to spin, or 'fish the bait' as the others put it. Worming, although a method allowed on some rivers in spate conditions, was not allowed on this particular fishery. I also learned that the salmon seems not to feed when in fresh water, but rather takes the fly or spoon out of some instinctive reaction to an intruder on its territory.

My borrowed tackle consisted of a Hardy Fibalite spinning rod of nine and a half feet, an Abu Ambassadeur multiplier reel, loaded with 18-pound Maxima nylon and a selection of Devon Minnows in a rather posh shoulder basket, or 'creel' as my host called it. Also in the creel were tins of swivels, weights and other oddments, and a wooden device with two metal 'eyes' that I subsequently discovered was to assist in the recovery of rock-bound tackle. It was an implement that came into much use during my first few hours on the river!

I had also borrowed a large salmon landing-net and a pair of chest-waders. My Barbour coat and trousers, and my priest were about the only trout gear that seemed appropriate to this type of game fishing and I was glad I had been able to borrow so much tackle. Buying it would have cost much more than my Rutland season ticket.

The fishery has a number of 'pools', or places where salmon rest up during their progress upriver to their spawning grounds. It was agreed that I should fish the pools below the fishing hut in the morning, then fish above the hut in the afternoon and evening. The angler sharing my stretch of the river decided to fish the upper four pools while I fished the lower pools and we were to change over at 11a.m. It all seemed very regular compared to the free-for-all on the trout lakes.

Although I was ably guided by the warden in the manner of casting and in the best places to cast, the first morning session was mainly spent in employing the wooden device with the metal 'eyes', that my ghillie called an 'otter', to extricate my line and Devon Minnow from submerged rocks – so much so, that at the time of our changeover I had only covered two of the four pools allocated to me. However, change over we did, and as I walked upstream to my next fishing position I remember reflecting that there was plenty of exercise to be had whilst salmon fishing, if not so many fish.

At about midday I was two or three paces down the third of my allocated pools and feeling pretty bored, I remember, with the whole thing. Suddenly, my line tightened. Almost at once the reel started to scream as a fish took off, downstream, with my Devon Minnow. Keeping my rod high, on the warden's instructions, I quickly tightened the tension on my reel to try to slow the fish down a bit. A few seconds later the reel stopped screaming and everything went solid.

'Keep a tight line and walk down to the fish', I was advised. I promptly obeyed and when I got level with the fish I started to apply some pressure. Nothing happened for what seemed an eternity, and I was just beginning to think I had fouled a rock and the fish was gone when, dramatically, the salmon started upriver and the reel sang again as another fifty yards of nylon cleared the spool.

Everything then went solid again. Back along the bank I trudged, not noticing how tired my arms were getting, I was so excited. Getting level with the fish again I kept a tight rein on the salmon as I reeled line in. Getting level with the fish once more, I tried to put some pressure on it. The rod bent double under the strain and I thought I'd definitely snagged this time. But no, after two minutes of putting intense pressure on rod, line and fish alike, the reel screamed out yet again as the salmon swam over to the other side of the river and settled there – solid, again, save for the light thumping feeling at the end of the line, as if the fish was swishing its tail to stay in its lie.

The fight continued for over an hour, by which time my arms felt as though they were about to drop off. Never once had I got a glimpse of the fish, although several times it had been right under my rod tip as I stood on the high bank over ten feet of water. It was at this point that the warden made what seemed to me the most obvious statement I had ever heard.

'It's a big fish, sir', he declared. It was only later that evening that I understood the significance of his observation, as I drowned my

Two Royal Deeside salmon for the author and his sister, Anna Graves

sorrows in then local hostelry along with the others on the beat, who
had also caught nothing. For, yes, after a battle lasting one and three-
quarter hours, the salmon finally got its freedom, as the knot attaching
the wooden bait to the line gave way. When he said my fish was a big
one, he meant I had been into a salmon of probably forty pounds.

Although I had caught many big-lake trout of over five pounds in
my angling career, nothing remotely approached the contest I had so
painfully lost with that salmon. The *fever* had struck!

Every year, since then, I've had a fresh attack. With my ever generous
brother-in-law providing the invitations I've fished several more times
on that stretch of the Wye – and on one memorable visit to Royal
Deeside to share a rod on a famous beat of the River Dee near Ballater.
It was here that I finally landed my first salmon, a silver beauty of
twelve pounds, fresh run from the sea, with lice all over it. What a
thrill. The photograph shows me and that salmon, with my sister Anna
Graves and one she caught from the same pool, within half-an-hour of
my capture. It's tremendously exhilarating to stand up to your waist,
in chest waders, with the force of the water threatening to sweep you
away in its swirling currents, as you cast your full fly-line across the
stream with a big double-handed rod, the mend of line to keep the fly
swimming smoothly past those rocky 'lies'; to then sense the excitement
as fly line and backing sail off your reel, as a salmon mouths your lure
and turns away downriver – steeling yourself, when your every sense
is telling you to strike, then, after what seems an eternity, the steady
lift of the rod, with hand on reel, to set the hook.

I've certainly no objection to anyone choosing to spin or worm for
salmon, when the rules permit, but for me the fly is the way I'd always
like to fish. Exercising control to delay the strike after the take, is for me,
the ultimate fly-fishing experience, followed very closely by the sheer
power the lordly salmon can exert in a fast-flowing river.

Good salmon fishing is, of course, generally expensive, some beats
costing as much per day as my Rutland season ticket. What's more, they
are often fully let, year in, year out. Some hotels have fishing rights that
they reserve exclusively for residents, but hotel accommodation is not
cheap any more. One place, however, where really good salmon fishing
can be had for the price of a trouting day permit, is Grantown-on-Spey,
in Scotland. I spent a week there recently and fished the thirty-one
pools of the Strathspey Angling Association on the famous River Spey
for less, per day, than it would have cost on a trout reservoir. The water
is well managed and offers fly-only fishing on some of its pools during
normal summer conditions. Tackle dealer Peter Hemmings, who runs
the Angus Stuart shop on Grantown's High Street, is a regular on the
water and will send you a map of the beat if you write to him. He
recommended me superb accommodation in an angler's guest house
in the town and supplied me with an armoury of 'local' flies at a very

reasonable price. His telephone number is 0479 2612. Go to his shop before you set foot on the river. He'll supply you with all the information you need, as to flies and lines to use and how to wade and fish the pools. Without his advice I would have been lost as a first-time visitor.

To fish the Association's water you have to be resident, if temporarily, in or in the vicinity of Grantown. Your weekly permit will allow you access to seven miles of the River Spey and twelve miles of one of its tributaries, the River Dulnain. About half of the Spey and most of the Dulnain is good fly water, although spinning and worming is allowed during high-water conditions. Although the Spey is noted as a famous salmon river, sea trout also begin to arrive, in quantity, from May onwards, providing excellent sport throughout the summer, particularly as darkness approaches. The River Spey is a wide waterway that demands deep wading in many of its pools to obtain best water coverage. As it is also one of the fastest flowing rivers in our country, standing waist deep in mid-stream is an extremely exciting experience, and I strongly recommend the use of a wading stick! Some of the pools have steep banks and others are tree lined so if, like me, you're a fly-only fisher you'll need to master the 'Spey cast' or 'double Spey cast' to fish these beats. Tuition is available locally or there are some excellent videos now on sale, which clearly define and demonstrate the methods. I found it almost impossible to practise until I got on the Spey, but took only a short while to become reasonably competent.

Finally, it should be stated that the Spey is also an excellent 'trout stream'. On my last day there a local angler landed a wild brownie, of over seven pounds, which took him more than an hour to subdue. For a long time he thought he'd hooked a good salmon. This fish came from the Nethy Pool at Nethybridge, a small village about five miles from Grantown. It's here that Dr John Bryden has a cottage to let on his farm, just two fields away from the Spey. This is ideal accommodation for a party of up to eight anglers who prefer self-catering, the friendly Rayburn stove offering excellent drying facilities as well as cooking the evening casserole while you're down by the river.

Unless I lived really close to a fine river like the Spey, I could never visualise salmon fishing replacing my love for the big lakes and the fine trout that flourish there. Knowing that trout feed avidly for much of the season at least gives me a chance of deceiving them now and again.

Yet somehow I know that at least once a year, salmon fever is likely to strike again. For all its frustrations, hunting those massive fish has an irresistible appeal that, sooner or later, has to be satisfied!

Chapter Ten

FIRST DAY FUN

If, like me, you spend November to March away from the lake, the first day of the new trout year is always something special to look forward to: an early opportunity to try out some of the flies created over hours at the tying vice while the white rime of hoar-frost cloaked our winter lawns.

The resident fish have had a few months to forget our many inexpert attempts to deceive them during the previous season. They will have been patrolling the margins, relatively undisturbed, for some time, joined now by hoards of smaller stockfish put in by thoughtful fishery managers for our continued pleasure. On the twenty-odd first days I can recall at least one exceptional trout has always been landed, and I know that next time it could be my turn to get the cameras clicking.

One disastrous year apart, my opening days have mostly been successful ones, with plenty of bag limits to please me and the friends who enjoy eating the fruits of my sport. This has been achieved by a combination of careful planning, thoughtful application of many skills acquired over long trouting experience, and not a little luck.

One year when everything went wrong was about five seasons after Grafham first opened. I had queued to get my permit in the early hours of the morning, and had set up camp on the upwind shore, near the Sailing Club. Fish had been showing in the area during the preceding week and I had secured a spot on a point which would give me several yards casting advantage over any anglers to my left or right. It was a cold night, with an increasing breeze at my back. I nestled down in my sleeping bag, under a large green coarse-fishing umbrella, and tried to get some rest. The fresh air nipped my nose with every breath.

As a storm threatened, the wind increased. I had no sooner reinforced the umbrella's anchorage, than a mixture of heavy rain and hail beat relentlessly on the canvas above my head. Cold, and damp, I tried in vain to get to sleep. After some time, and for no apparent reason, the wind changed right round, through almost a hundred and eighty degrees, toppling my umbrella and ripping it from the ground. My sleeping bag became soaked as I clambered to my feet, to rescue my shelter.

I was not amused, and now I was in a dilemma. Should I stay and hope the wind would change back again, or should I collect everything together and move to the opposite bank? Looking round my considerable collection of tackle and clothing by torchlight, I decided to stay put until the morning and made a fresh camp as best I could.

The cold northerly wind had now reached gale force. It was about the worst night I can ever remember enduring. When it finally got light enough to see, I could tell there was no point in staying. The waves were crashing into the shore in front of me and the water would soon be brown with suspended sand for as far as I could cast.

It took me some time to pack up my gear and drive round to the North Shore. When I arrived I was not surprised to see anglers every fifteen yards or so, all along the back-wind shoreline. Determined to find somewhere to fish, I set off along the line of fishermen to look for a reasonable space to cast. Every now and then a rod would bend to indicate that trout were feeding. I eventually found a spot that had just been vacated by a disappointed angler, who told me he hadn't had a pull in two hours.

'And I haven't had a cast, yet', I remember saying to myself.

For what seemed an eternity I did everything I could think of to get an offer, all to no avail. I had just made my umpteenth change of fly, when a young man started to wade into the water, no more than five or six yards to my left. Dressed in a crease-free Barbour and bright green waders, this obvious newcomer to our sport began to thrash around, his brightly varnished rod flashing in the sunlight. His fly line hit the water in front of and behind him with a splish, splash, reminiscent, I remembered, of my own first attempts at casting.

His pal, clearly a fisher of more experience, waded in on my right-hand side, only some ten yards away and commenced to shout instructions to the novice, right across my swim! After a short time, and just as I had cast a long line, an explosive commotion came from my left-hand side. The gleaming Bruce and Walker of our new-found colleague was bent into a trout which, because of a bird's-nest tangle in between the top eyes of his rod, could only leap up and down in the water on its tight rein.

'I've got one, Harry! I've got one Harry!' the flawless Barbour called to his mate, who promptly, and without consideration, crashed out of the water on my right, and, with a similar disturbance, splashed into the water to my left to help his friend, scooping up the fish, a rainbow of about two and a half pounds, in his net as it made its twentieth leap for freedom.

Not believing what I had just witnessed, I put my rod over my shoulder and turned to wade to the bank. You've guessed it. As I approached the shore, the rod was almost wrenched from my grasp as a rainbow tugged at my Sweeney Todd lure, and broke free. Quickly reeling in my line, I looked at my flyless leader and decided enough was enough!

I have, of course, had plenty of 'blanks' since that one, but none I remember so vividly.

However, I did learn from that experience. I now never go trout fishing without phoning for a weather forecast beforehand. In advance of a bank-fishing excursion, I try to choose likely spots to fish by studying a map of the water in relation to the winds that have been prevailing in the area during the preceding few days. Early season, I'll choose a point on an upwind shore, where I'll get a slight cross-breeze, from right to left if possible, to allow me to retrieve my fly with the underwater current. Trout tend to reside on the warmer upwind shore during the first few weeks of the season, and if I can get a light ripple crossing in front of me, it helps work my flies in an enticing arc on retrieval.

If you get a prior opportunity to visit the venue you choose for your first day 'fling', take it. Ask any locals you meet, where trout have been 'showing' recently. Seek out anglers in a nearby pub. Try to find out where new stock-fish have been introduced. These 'stockies' often stimulate feeding activity amongst the overwintered trout. If you can walk the shore at dusk, you may well spot feeding activity in the margins. Use any information gleaned to plan, with the help of the previous day's weather forecast, which spots to fish. List them in order of priority, because you'll be lucky, indeed, to find your first choice free on the morrow.

If you decide to camp out overnight in order to ensure your choice of swim, take a leaf out of the survival book and include in your kit a large plastic bag. Even in the relative comfort of a car it can be really cold during the night in late March. I've several times had ice on the inside of the car windows whilst waiting for first light on opening day. You'll be surprised how warm a plastic bag will keep you, even in those conditions.

Another thing which will help make your day is the means to cook yourself a hot breakfast. A small bottled-gas ring and a frying pan sizzling with fried bacon and mushrooms is guaranteed to warm a cold stomach and turn every head as the cooking smells waft along the shoreline. A little kettle or saucepan will also enable you to brew up when sport slows.

So far as tackle is concerned, I usually start by making up a rod with an Intermediate line, a cast of about fifteen feet of 6lb Drennan Double Strength nylon and a plain black lure, with a marabou wing. If you are fishing back-wind, remember the underwater current will be coming towards you. Since trout in cold water seem to respond best to slowly moving food forms, this is the way to start. Cast out and begin retrieving in slow, figure-of-eight movements, interspersed with the odd pause for a second or two. Next cast, if you didn't get a take on your first, count to five before retrieving, and so on until you snag bottom. Then start over again. If you get an offer, remember the depth you were fishing at and repeat the medicine.

If no interest is aroused with the Intermediate line, try a Wetcel 1 slow-sinker. Your failure to catch is far more likely to be due to the wrong depth than to the colour or type of lure used. Start, as you did with the Intermediate, by retrieving straight away on the first cast, after a five second pause on the next and so on until you snag up. Then start over again. It's hard to imagine a situation where these two lines prove inadequate from the early season shore, so if you haven't caught after two hours, I suggest you move to another area and try the same techniques there.

If you spot any flies around during the midday period, try fishing a floater with a team of nymphs for a while. Put on a leader of about eighteen feet of 6lb Drennan Double Strength nylon, with droppers at eight feet and twelve feet from the point. For optimum strength, a dab of super-glue should be put on the dropper knots. I like a No. 14 buoyant pheasant-tail on the top dropper, a No. 12 pheasant-tail on the middle and, at this time of the year, a No. 10 leaded pheasant-tail on the point. Cast out and tuck your rod under your arm to let everything settle. But be vigilant. Takes often come whilst doing nothing, or 'on the drop', as I call it. When you do decide to retrieve, do it very slowly indeed, stopping frequently for a second or two. This is my favourite way of fishing, but I have to say I don't catch many trout on the first day in this manner. So, if after half an hour the method hasn't worked for you, get back to your sunk line and lure again.

If you're starting early on the first day, beware of frost. Sometimes this can freeze up your rod rings after the initial wetting of the line, with potentially disastrous results.

Fishing at Rutland a few years ago, that first-day frost was really severe. We'd slept overnight in my pal's car, the windows of which had a thick layer of ice on the inside when we eventually decided it was time to get down to the water side.

It was still moonlight outside, and the road was slippery with rime as we made our way to the dam, where we'd decided to fish in the east-north-easterly breeze that prevailed. It was freezing hard, nipping our noses and numbing our fingers as we made up our rods in the half-light. I put on a slow-sinking Wetcel 1 with fifteen feet of Drennan Double Strength and a red chenille lure with a black marabou wing and grey squirrel over-wing. Its silver ribbing was hardly discernible in the pale light of dawn.

I decided to start fishing without delay, and cast a longish line out into the gloom, retrieving very slowly, and pausing every now and then before continuing to draw in line with a figure-of-eight hand movement. The next cast didn't work and I realised my fly line had stuck in my top rod rings, with ice. Dipping the rod under the surface and casting again, quickly, I managed another fairly long line. This time I counted to five before starting my retrieve and was straight away into a fish. Even as I played it I had to keep dipping the top of my rod beneath the water to keep the rod rings free. I netted and despatched the silver stocky, of about a pound and a quarter.

'What did you get it on?' my pal called.

'Red lure', I replied. 'Would you like one?'

'Thanks', he replied and I walked over the rocky dam wall to his swim, fly box under my arm, slipping and sliding as I went.

'Fish it slow, and count down to five before retrieving', I advised, handing over a replica of the lure I was fishing and knowing he, too, was using a Wetcel 1 line.

I stood and watched my pal cast, after dipping his rod, and as I waited for him to start retrieving, I noticed how cold my hands were. Half-way through his retrieve, his line tightened and he was into another lively little rainbow.

'They don't seem to mind the cold', I mused, as I waited with his net for the short battle to end. 'I've got a feeling we're going to clean up this morning.'

I walked back to my own swim. My rod rings were solid with ice when I got back, and it took several dips in the water to free them sufficiently to be able to cast. Counting to five, again, I looked at my pal, who was beating his chest with his arms to keep warm.

'It's enough to freeze the . . .'

I never finished the sentence. A heavy thumping at the end of my line indicated that this was a better fish that I'd hooked, and possibly a brownie. As I made line on the fish, I bent to pick up my landing net from the rock beside me. It wouldn't budge. The frost had stuck it firmly to the stone dam-wall and no amount of tugging on my part would loosen it.

'Lend me your net, Ian', I called. 'Mine's stuck to the rocks.'

The brownie, a fish of about two pounds, was on its side. I brought it in towards me, rod held high, and, gripping the red lure with frozen finger and thumb, freed it from the trout's scissors with a sharp twist. Holding it gently, upright, I let it slide slowly back into the depths, none the worse for its ordeal.

'Might get to be a ten pounder', I explained to my mate. 'I'm going to put all small browns back, this year!'

I freed my landing net, by tipping water all over it, and stood it upright to keep it free from the rocks.

Ian and I had 'limited' by eight o'clock and retired to the fishing lodge for a toasted bacon sandwich and a hot cup of coffee, by which time the sun was rising and steam exuded from the Whitwell Creek as the temperature also rose. It had been a cold start to the season, but one of the more successful ones we could remember.

On the first day that Rutland Water opened for trout fishing, we'd spent the night on the bank at the end of the Hambleton Peninsula. It had been a sleepless one due, mainly, to the fact that all night we could hear trout sipping earthworms from the edge of the water, at our feet. Every time it happened, my pal Ian said, loudly, 'Bloody Hell, did you hear that?' It was hard to tell who was the most excited, him or me!

Every now and then we'd have other anglers walking past our pitch, looking for somewhere to fish. It was a dark night, I remember, and Ian and I were in sleeping bags, side-by-side in a huge plastic bag which we'd had made up for us at work. Our other two pals, Peter and Graham, had retired from the bank to sleep in Pete's car, at the top of the hill. Graham could never stand the cold of the night lake-shore.

I must have dozed off eventually, because the next thing I knew was Pete's voice from the water, shouting.

'I'm in! I'm In!'

He had, unknown to Ian and I, crept down to the lake, still well before dawn and the official opening time, and had waded in to cast the first line. On his first cast he'd had what may well have been the first trout caught from that marvellous fishery.

His shout had woken every bank angler on Hambleton, it seemed, and the next thing I heard was the sound of lines swishing back and forth everywhere.

I scrambled out of my sleeping bag, only to remember I was still in my vest and pants. I'd stripped down earlier, because I'd got too hot with all my clothes on. Now, here I was, struggling to find my trousers in the dark, whilst, all round, reels were screaming as angler after angler got into a trout.

Anyway, we all had a good time that morning and as sport subsided with the rising sun, Ian and I decided to head for the fishing lodge and the shower room, to freshen up.

The lodge was newly built and the showers looked inviting with their sparkling new tiles and taps. As usual, Ian was undressed and under one of them while I was still getting off my pullover. Grabbing a bar of soap from one of the wash-hand basins, he turned on the shower dial and started to soap himself all over, hair and all. When he had got a superb lather everywhere and was still rubbing the soapy bar all over his chest and stomach, the water from the shower-head eased to a slow drip. He looked up at that shower-head in disbelief, like a snowman watching the sun come up!

'Bloody shower's stopped', he swore, and dived under the next one. After a little trickle, that one too reverted to a drip. To the next shower,

Ian rushed, with the same result. 'Christ!' he exclaimed. 'The bloody water's stopped everywhere!'

I couldn't see for laughing. I fell about. I have never in my life seen such a comic figure, nor ever seen Ian in such panic!

He stood there, hands cupped under the shower-head. Drip, drip, the water slowly made a small puddle in his hand. Then, swoosh, he threw the small pool over his chest and private parts in an abortive effort to clear the suds from his naked torso.

When I'd recovered my composure a little, and thanking myself for not having rushed to the shower as Ian had done, I said, weakly, 'Try the wash-hand basin.'

These basins at Rutland are the first thing you see when you enter the gents in the lodge. Ian turned on the taps and water rushed out of the cold one only. The hot tap was empty. Ian's language was unprintable as he sploshed this cold water all over himself. He made a pretty sight, bent forward over the wash-hand basin as he was, his black-haired bum in full view.

Suddenly, the door opened behind him and a tall, arrogant looking chap stood there, impeccably attired in plus-fours, Harris jacket and deerstalker, his face incredulous with astonishment.

'Oh, my God!' he said, in a beautiful Oxford accent, and slammed the door shut as he beat a hasty retreat.

I laughed tears, and was still laughing when Ian ultimately got himself clear enough of suds to towel himself down.

The day ended with our clean hero back on Hambleton point, netting the last trout of his limit as the sun set in a fire-streaked sky behind us.

Whatever you do, have fun on your next First Day. It's great to be back in action again, and, who knows, that record trout might still be yours at the end of the session.

Chapter Eleven

TROUT FISHING ETIQUETTE

It had been a blissful morning. The shadowy wisp of dawn had faded as the sun rose, bright, behind us. The gentle ripple danced its sparkling way across the lake and the gentle throb of an engine heralded the arrival of the first boat-anglers. The peaceful hour of trout fishing, on Grafham's dam that my colleagues and I had just enjoyed, was about to end, abruptly.

As the boat and its three occupants got nearer I had the premonition that these were not your average trout fishermen. Their raucous laughter could be heard two hundred yards away, and I thought they seemed more like soccer lager-louts than anglers.

My concentration on the approaching craft was broken when I noticed the angler beside me strike into a fish, then watched his rod arch, his reel screaming, as a good rainbow headed for the lake. Next thing I knew, my own rod was nearly wrenched from my hands as another trout smashed at my Green and Brown nymphs and, hooking itself, bored deep.

It took me only a minute or two to subdue and net the suicidal small brownie, which I judged to be about a pound and a quarter as I gently lowered him back into the water. I knew this was breaking the rule of the fishery, but I somehow have never had the heart to kill these little fellows, knowing their longevity and the formidable quarry they make when three or four years old. Fortunately, fishery managers are now more enlightened and most encourage the return of small stock-browns.

The chap to my left was still struggling with his own fish and I went along the wall to offer assistance with the net. As I watched him playing the lively rainbow, I noticed the boat of three had changed course and was heading straight for us. It was only a hundred yards away when first an empty crisp packet, and then the wrapping from a cigarette carton, went over the side. I netted the rainbow, a lovely, deep hen-fish of about two and three-quarter pounds and carried it back up the wall, towards the man's tackle bags. The fish was despatched and we exchanged a few pleasantries, our backs to the lake.

Deciding to get back to my own swim, I turned to walk away, and noticed that the boat had now dropped anchor, right in front of my colleague's pitch and only about thirty yards out. I was about half-way back to my tackle when the chap behind me shouted, quite politely I thought, 'Do you mind keeping your distance?' He had obviously turned to see the anchored boat in his swim!

The reply from one of the boat's occupants was totally unprintable. Then, from another of the three, 'P'raps he wants all the . . . lake!'

By this time the angler to the left of the fracas joined in.

'. . . off, or I'll fetch the bailiffs!'

Then the occupant at the engine end of the boat stood up and turned round to face the dam.

'Shut your . . . face or I'll come and spank your arse', the burly individual shouted.

Realising the futility of the slanging match, the angler to my left picked up his rod and creel and walked towards me and a clear swim, a hundred yards to my right.

'Nice lot', he said, simply, as he walked by. I know how he felt.

On another occasion, at Rutland, I had anchored my boat in a heavy swell, off one of the Normanton points. I was close to the shore, there being no bank-anglers. The strong westerly wind was setting up fast underwater currents that were sweeping over this particular point, a shallow area near the Normanton ticket office. The swim was alive with trout of a good average size, and we were having a field-day with our leaded Green and Brown nymphs. It wasn't long, however, before we were joined by an armada of boats. You would have thought it was the only place that held any fish on the 3,200 acres of that lake!

First we had a drifting boat, its occupants fishing loch-style, come very close to our left. Despite the fact that their boat was moving diagonally, they continued their drift. The boat passed across our swim, only thirty-five yards downwind of us, completely cutting off our 'takes' for half an hour. The next incident was worse.

We'd just got the trout going again when a boat tried to anchor, about twenty yards behind us and to our left, with one of the fishery's own anchors, which were pretty useless at the time, let alone in a gale. They had even tried to tether the boat broadside, against the wind. Of course, the inevitable happened and the boat simply drifted towards us. Pleased to be getting nearer the action, the two occupants of the boat carried on casting and the next thing I knew a big white lure plopped into the water only five yards in front of me and slightly to my left. I must admit I felt like turning round and giving the occupants a piece of well-chosen advice. Instead I turned to my companion and said, quietly, 'We seem to have attracted them all, today.'

'Bunch of . . .' was my mate's bawdy reply.

Anyway, the boat had just got alongside our own, when one of the occupants started pulling on the anchor rope, to lift it, whilst the other began pulling the engine starter-string. After several attempts the engine roared into life, the throttle wide open, spray flying everywhere, right where a few minutes previously I'd hooked a nice rainbow. Muttering something that sounded like 'Sorry . . .', the chap at the engine end threw the boat into gear, noisily, and powered away leaving our swim a boil of churning, swirling water.

We moved then ourselves, my pal swearing profusely about his day being ruined. Actually it wasn't. We re-anchored near the Bunds in the afternoon and bagged up in less than an hour, with three two-pound-plus fish in our bags. Naturally, we reported the boat number to the wardens when we left the lake, and I've no doubt they spoke to the anglers about their indiscretion, but that knowledge didn't really compensate for the problems we'd experienced earlier. The fishery has now provided much better anchors in the boats, but the ropes could be longer.

It's a pity that more space isn't given to articles on fishing etiquette in our widely-read monthlies. They seem to avoid the subject, regarding practical fishing articles as more important. Perhaps it is, if you want to sell monthlies.

Increasingly we see evidence of discord between bank-anglers and boats, between traditional boat-fishing and the Northampton-style exponents, and between boats wishing to anchor and those preferring to drift-fish. For God's sake, what is going on? The waters, generally, are big enough to support all the forms of our sport. If they aren't the fishery management on those lakes should set some rules.

We've so far discussed the problems that exist between boats and bank-anglers and between boats and other boats. What about the problems between bank-angler and fellow bank-angler and between fishermen sharing the same boat?

A few years ago now I was fishing with an old work colleague on the 'boil' at Grafham, that turmoil of water caused by the pumping of water into the reservoir from the Great Ouse river. We had had a successful few hours, which accounted for the enthusiasm of my boat partner. Anyway, I'd cast out, well over the turmoil of the water inlet-pipe and had counted my ten-yard lead-core shooting-head down to thirty-five. This was the known distance of the 'taking depth' on that day. Tucking my rod under my arm, I'd begun, very slowly, retrieving my cast of three pheasant-tail nymphs. Suddenly, my rod top curved downwards, and I instinctively tightened into the heaviest fish I have ever hooked in a big lake. I battled hard with my rod and line to make an impression on the deeply-boring fish in the heavy currents of the boil, as my boat partner retrieved his line and lure from the depths. I couldn't move the fish even with my rod bent in a full arc. Then, to my horror, my colleague cast his heavy line across the swim again. I tried to put side strain on the fish to bring it away from the boil,

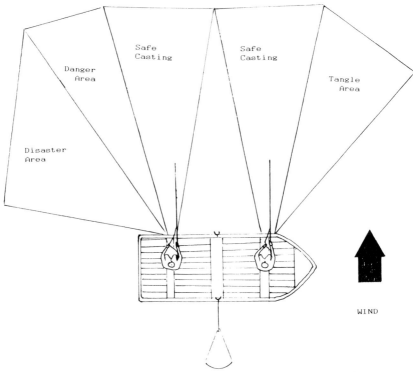

Two right-handers in a boat, showing the casting areas for safe or dangerous fishing

and his lead-core line. Still I made no impression on it. Off it went again, on another powerful run, then, slack line, and I knew that it was gone.

On retrieval, I found my eight-pound leader broken. My pal's heavy line had crossed mine, putting extra pressure on already strained tackle and the worst had happened. At first I thought it could have been a pike, but there was no frayed leader where it had broken. No, I really believe I was into a monster brownie that day and I've never really forgiven my old friend for his unethical behaviour.

If you're in a boat, and your partner is into a fish, the gentlemanly way is to retrieve your own line as quickly as possible, stow your rod in the boat and take up the landing net to boat your partner's fish. Only when his trout is safely in the boat, should you continue with your own fishing. Never, ever start to cast whilst your boat partner is playing a fish. Even if it doesn't lose him his trout, it puts him under more pressure than is necessary. Anyway, it's the height of bad manners.

If both anglers in the boat cast with the same hand, the one casting over his partner should never do so in a manner that might endanger or distress his colleague. The line drawings show the dangerous and no-go areas of cast. Avoid these areas at all cost, and especially if you're not insured. Watch your partner casting and try to ensure that *your* cast occurs, whilst your colleague is retrieving. Never cast across his line, whatever the temptation. It is only ethical to cast over to his side of the boat if he's got his line out of the water and isn't ready to cast. Learn to cast overhead properly, then even three can fish with equanimity and accord.

It's all common sense, really. Imagine your boat partner is a prospective father-in-law, whom you want to impress with your good manners. Try to make him comfortable in every way and help him to enjoy his day to the full. Remember, unless disability prevents it, the man not on the engine handles the anchor and the drogue. If you're fishing Northampton style, share the engine end, where all the work is done. Always offer to net your boat partner's trout.

If you're bank-fishing, adopt a gentlemanly attitude to other bank anglers. Never, ever encroach too close to another trouter. As a rule of thumb guide, you should allow at least twenty yards between anglers, thirty yards, if possible. Always enter, and leave, the water with as little disturbance as possible, not only for your own sake, but so as not to cause annoyance to your neighbouring fisher. If you see him into a good fish, offer to net it for him. If the angler in the next swim asks for your successful pattern, give him a truthful reply and tell him the line you're fishing and the depth you're fishing at. Offer him a similar fly, if you have one. If he then catches, his day will be made, and so, my friend, will yours. Enabling a fellow angler to catch is the most satisfying experience in trouting and one which I strongly recommend to you.

We need, desperately, to get back to accepting some of the old values that used to prevail in trout fishing. They amount to consideration for the sport, whether or not we agree with the methods being employed, and of our fellow trouter. His comfort and his solitude, should be preserved, wherever possible. Assistance should be offered to the inexperienced, even if this means giving up some of your own time. Criticism inhibits learning but good advice, genuinely offered, will almost always result in better behaviour in the future.

If fishery managements spent more time educating their regular customers, as well as the newcomers to our sport, in trout-fishing etiquette, it would bring benefits all-round. A happy pastime is a popular pastime.

So there you have it. If you've enjoyed reading this book as much as I've enjoyed writing it, my task has been achieved. I wish you many tight lines and leviathans to net.

See you on the lake!

Trouting should be a relaxing experience!